Portland and Newboro Ontario in Colour Photos, Saving Our History One Photo at a Time

Photography
by Barbara Raué
2016

Series Name:
Cruising Ontario

Book 160: Portland and Newboro

Cover photo: 7 Drummond Street, Newboro, Page 33

Series Name: Cruising Ontario
Saving Our History One Photo at a Time
in colour photos

Books Available in Alphabetical Order:
Aberfoyle, Acton, Alton, Amherstburg, Ancaster, Arthur, Aylmer, Ayr, Bloomingdale, Brantford, Burlington, Caledon, Caledonia, Cambridge, Clifford, Conestogo, Delhi, Dorchester to Aylmer, Drayton, Drumbo, Dundas, Eden Mills, Elmira, Elora, Essex, Fergus, Guelph, Hagersville, Hamilton, Hanover, Harriston, Hespeler, Jarvis, Kingston, Kingsville, Kitchener, Linwood, Listowel, London, Lucknow, Mono, Mount Forest, Neustadt, New Hamburg, Niagara-on-the-Lake, Oakville, Orangeville, Orillia, Owen Sound, Palmerston, Peterborough, Petrolia, Port Elgin, Preston, Rockwood, Sarnia, Seaforth, Sheffield, Shelburne, Simcoe, Southampton, St. Jacobs, St. Marys, St. Thomas, Stoney Creek, Stratford, Thamesford, Tillsonburg, Waterdown, Waterford, Waterloo, Welland, Wellesley, Windsor, Wingham, Woodstock

Other Books by Barbara Raue

Coins of Gold

Arrows, Indians and Love

The Life and Times of Barbara
Volume 1: Inventions That Have Enhanced My Life
Volume 2: Entertainment That I Have Enjoyed
Volume 3: East Coast Trips
Volume 4: Olympics Have Always Intrigued Me
Volume 5: Wonders of the World
Volume 6: Caribbean Cruises We Have Enjoyed
Volume 7: Animals
Volume 8: Storms and Other Major Disasters in My Lifetime
Volume 9: Wars, Terrorist Attacks and Major Disasters

The Cromwell Family Book

Laura Secord Discovered

Daddy Where Are You?

Montana Series
Book 1: Montana Dream
Book 2: Life on the Montana Frontier
Book 3: Montana to Boston and Back

Visit Barbara's website to view all of her books
http://barbararaue.ca

Table of Contents

Portland is a community located in Eastern Ontario within the township of Rideau Lakes in the United Counties of Leeds and Grenville. It is north of Kingston and situated on Big Rideau Lake.

Portland was first settled in the early nineteenth century as one of the first settlements along the Rideau Waterway. With the completion of the Rideau Canal Waterway in 1832, steamboats and barges carried raw materials such as cordwood, maple syrup, potash, cheese, tanned hides and salt beef. Portland became a thriving village of trade with Kingston, Montreal and Ottawa.

The village of Portland took its name in 1843 from William Cavendish-Bentinck, 3rd Duke of Portland, a British Whig and Tory statesman, Chancellor of the University of Oxford, and served as Prime Minister of Great Britain in 1783 and Prime Minister of the United Kingdom from 1807 to 1809.

By the 1860s, the settlement had expanded considerably to require five hotels and, by the early twentieth century, cottages were built around the lake and the tourist trade began. Advances in rail and road travel and increasing tourism offset a decline in the role of agriculture in the economy of Portland. Tourism began to lead the economy and still does to this day.

An international speed skating tournament called Skate the Lake is held each winter on the Big Rideau Lake at Portland.

The settlement of this area was begun during the construction of the Rideau Canal in 1826-32. A major construction camp was located here at the Isthmus between the Rideau and Mud (Newboro) Lakes. In 1833, Benjamin Tett, owner of a nearby sawmill, opened a store and three years later a post office named Newborough was established. A small community including several stores developed as a trade center for the region's lumbering industry and agriculture. About 1850 a tannery was established and within ten years two iron mines were opened. The ore was exported via the Rideau to smelters in the United States. A foundry and a steam sawmill stimulated growth.

In 1888, a branch of the Brockville-Westport & S.S.M. Railroad came to Newboro. Trade and travel were now year-round. Produce of local farm and forest entered wider markets through Newboro's cannery and mills. From Newboro Station, local scholars went to and from high school in Athens and Brockville.

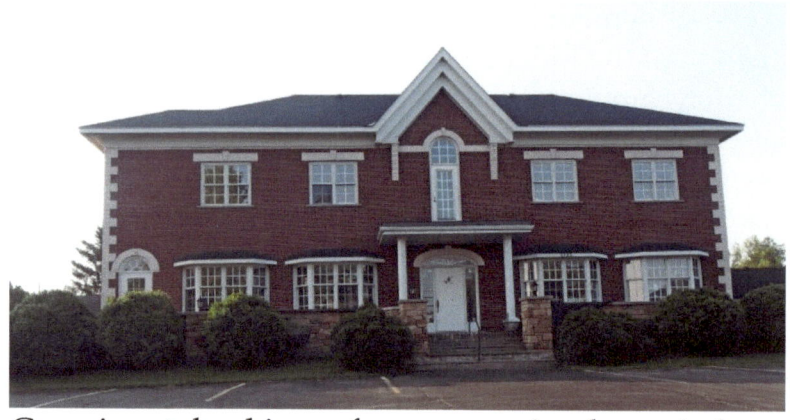

Georgian style - hip roof, corner quoins, bay windows

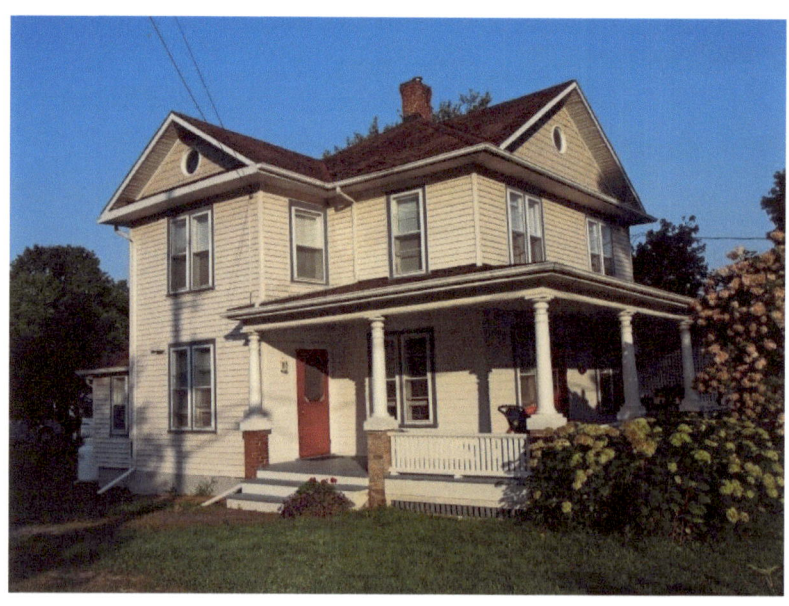

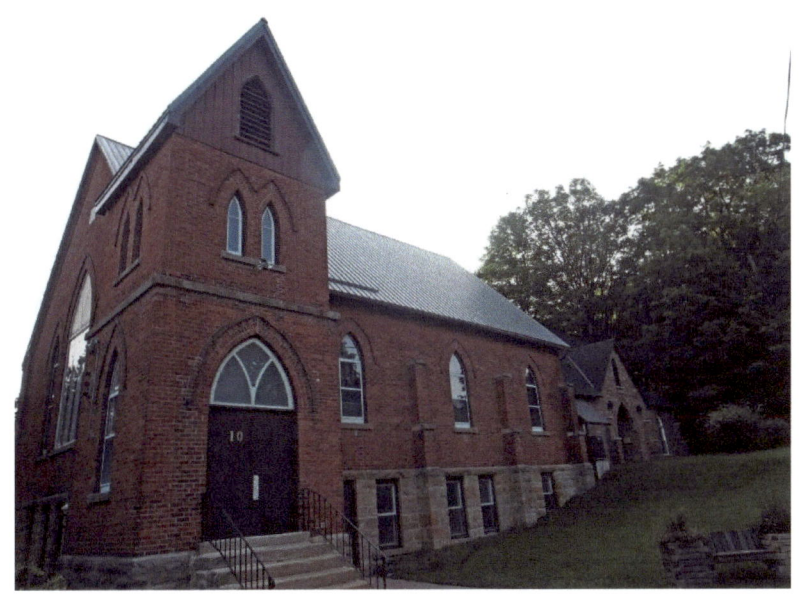

Portland United Church – Gothic Revival – lancet windows, banding, buttresses

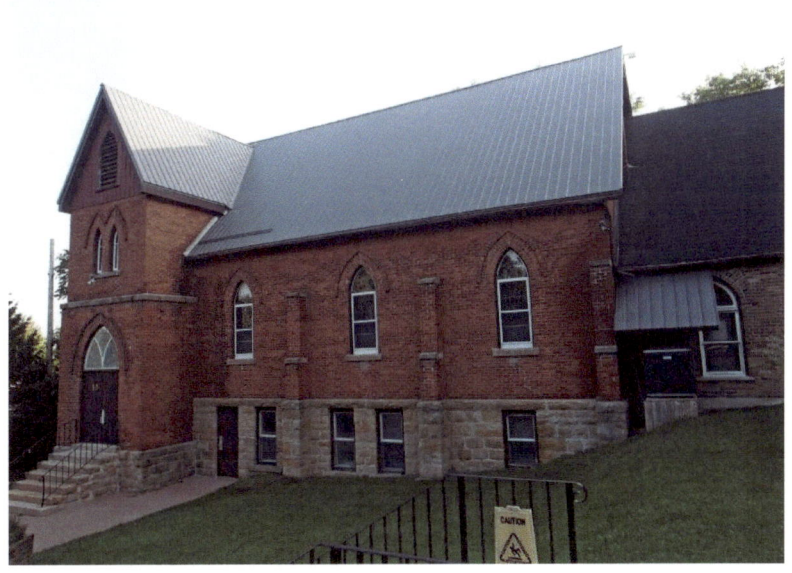

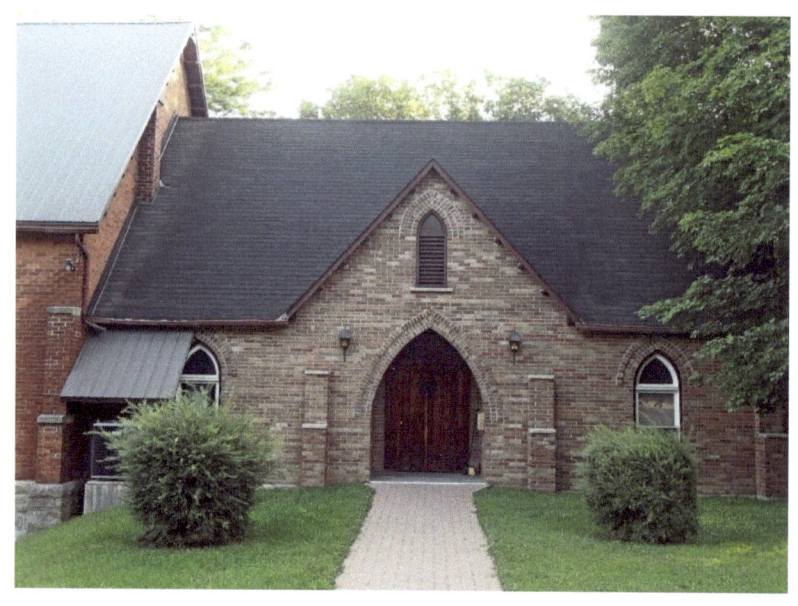

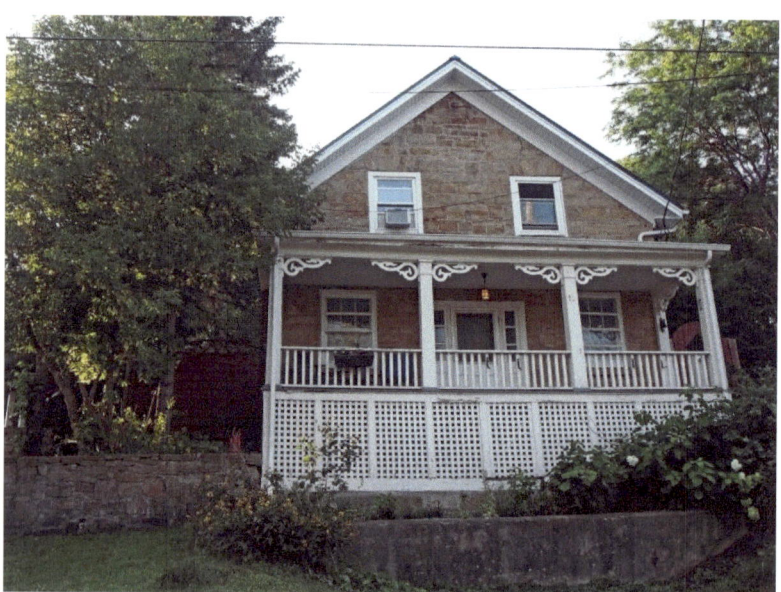

12 Colborne Street – John Grant House – c. 1872 – sandstone –
Ontario Cottage – bric-a-brac on porch pillars

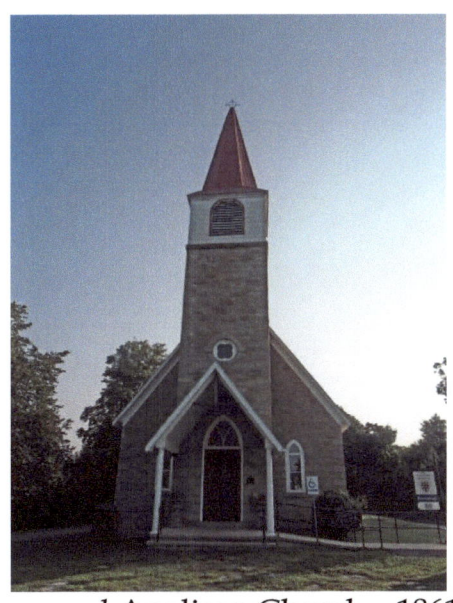

Portland Emmanuel Anglican Church – 1861 – Cambrian sandstone – buttresses, stained glass windows, lancet windows

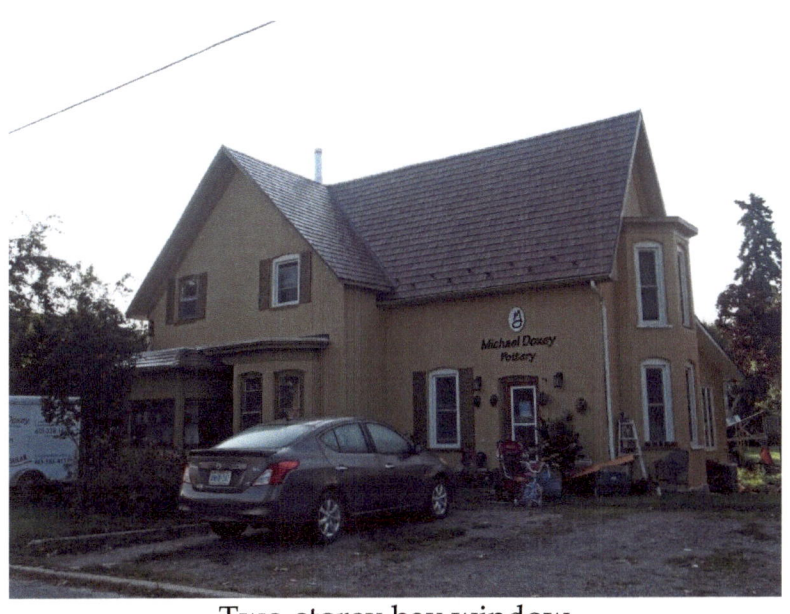

Two-storey bay window

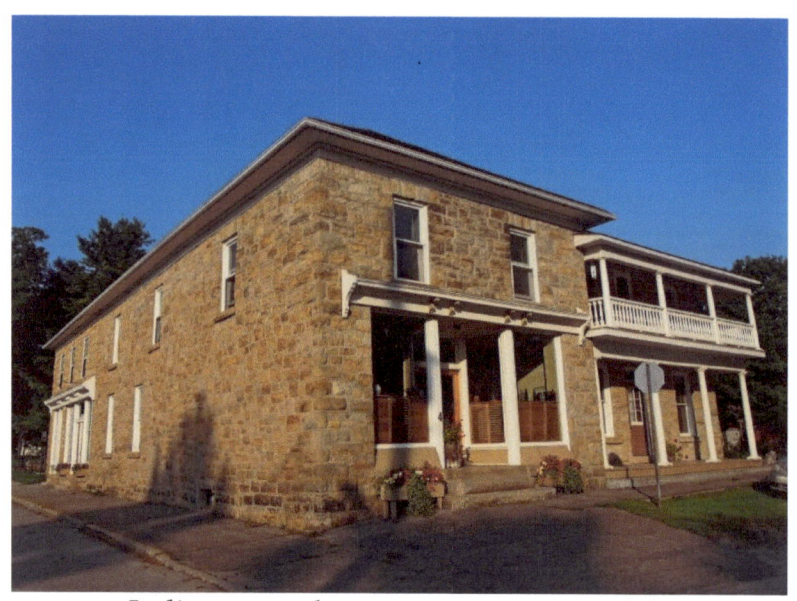

Italianate style – two-storey verandah

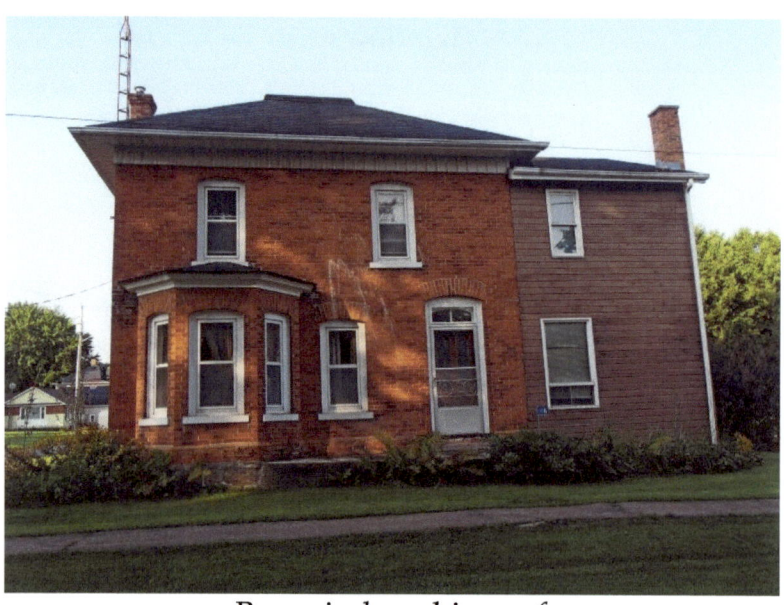

Bay window, hip roof

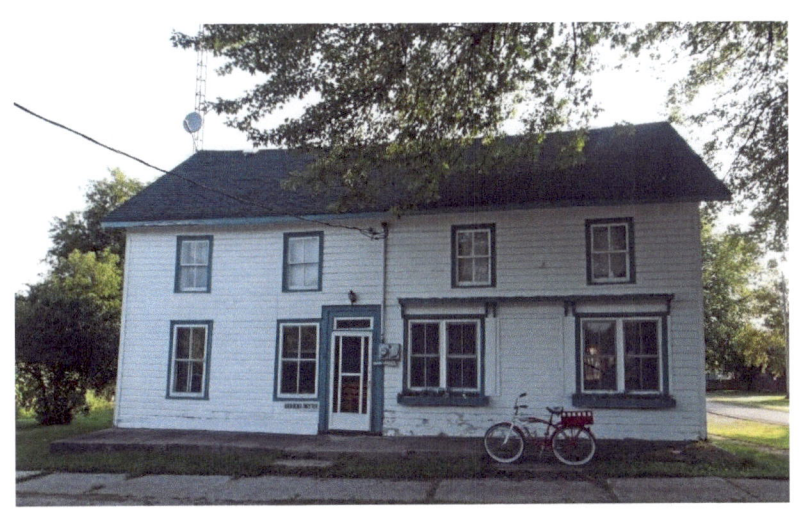

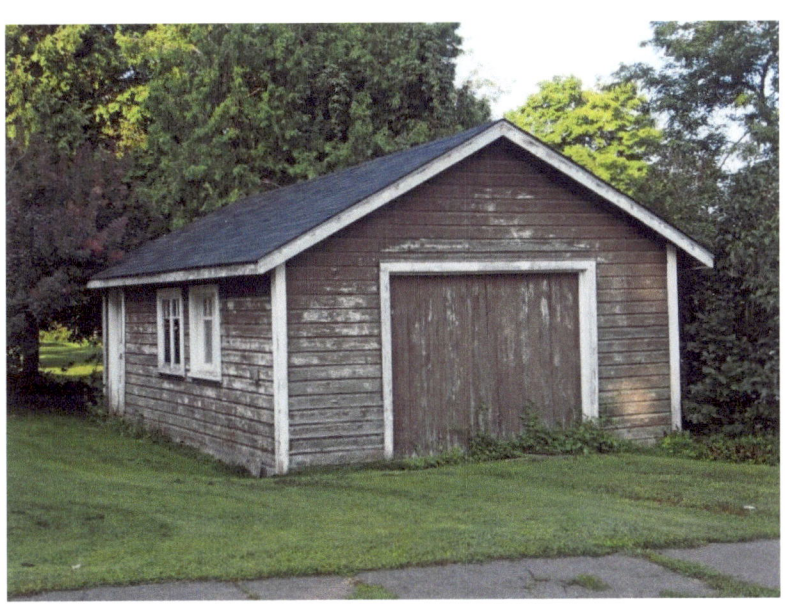

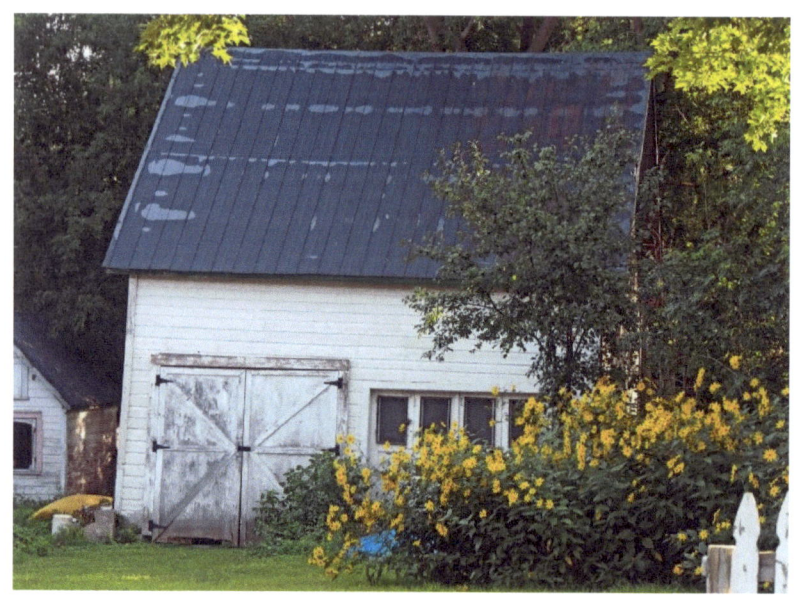

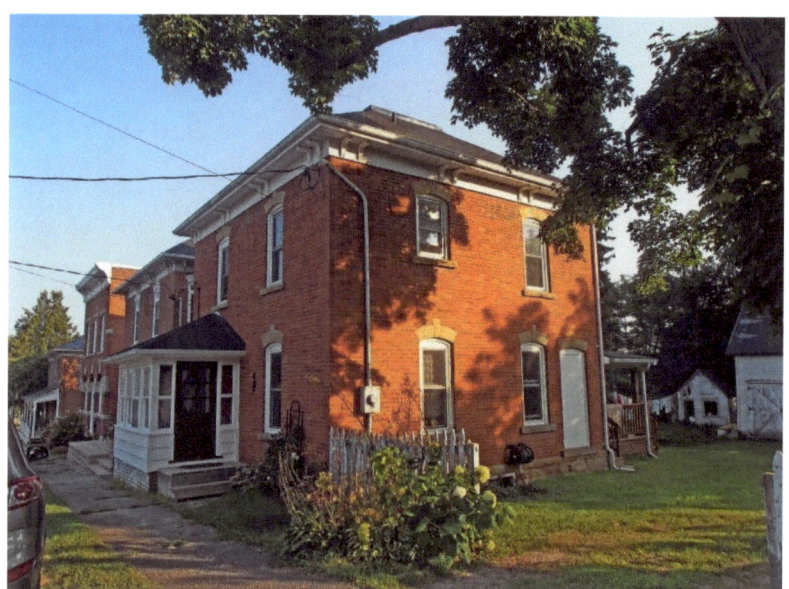

Italianate – paired cornice brackets, voussoirs, keystones

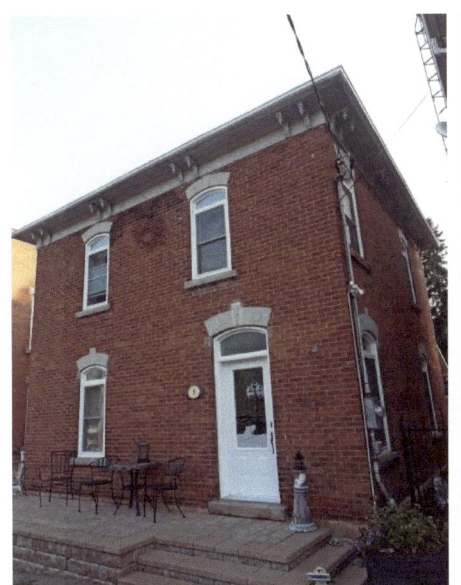

Cornice brackets

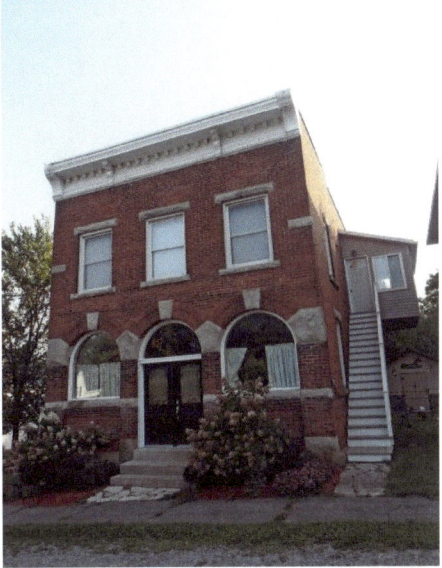

Dentil molding and brackets
Large keystones, even larger
stones at the base of the voussoirs

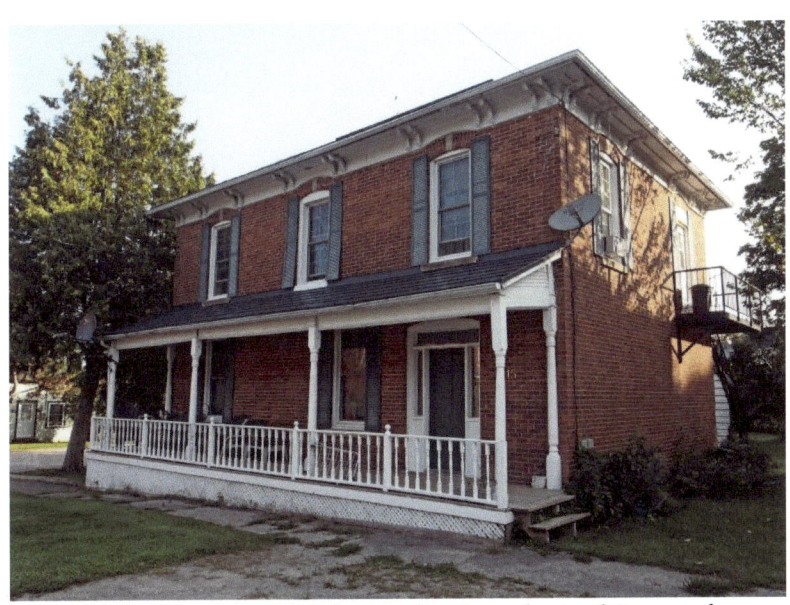

Italianate – paired cornice brackets, hip roof

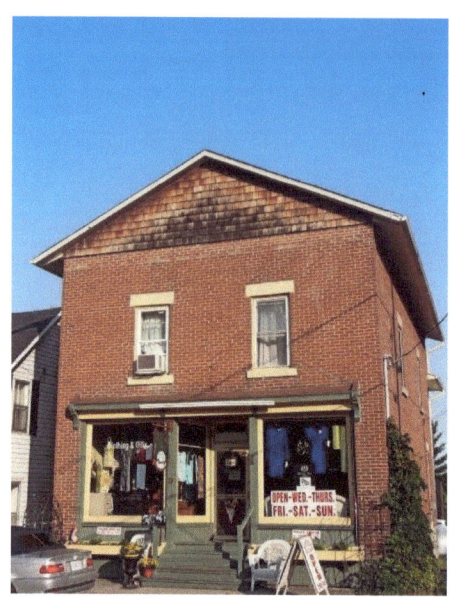

Edwardian style

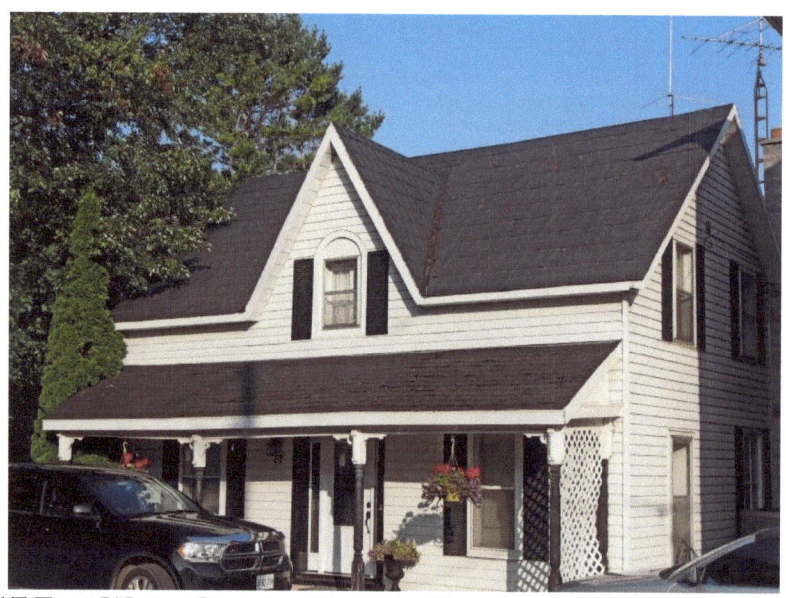

17 East Water Street – Ontario Cottage style – Peter Cole house – 1850s – front gable window with a semi-circular head; veranda across the front facade

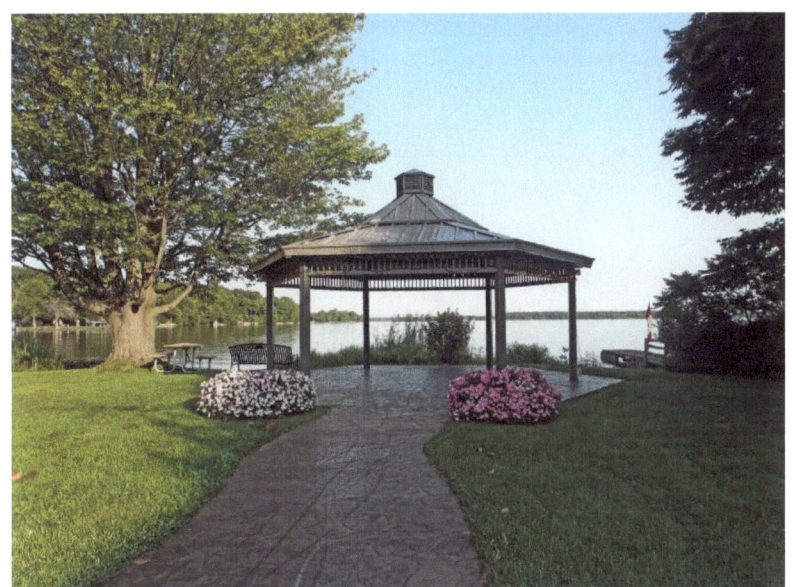

Gazebo on Great Rideau Lake

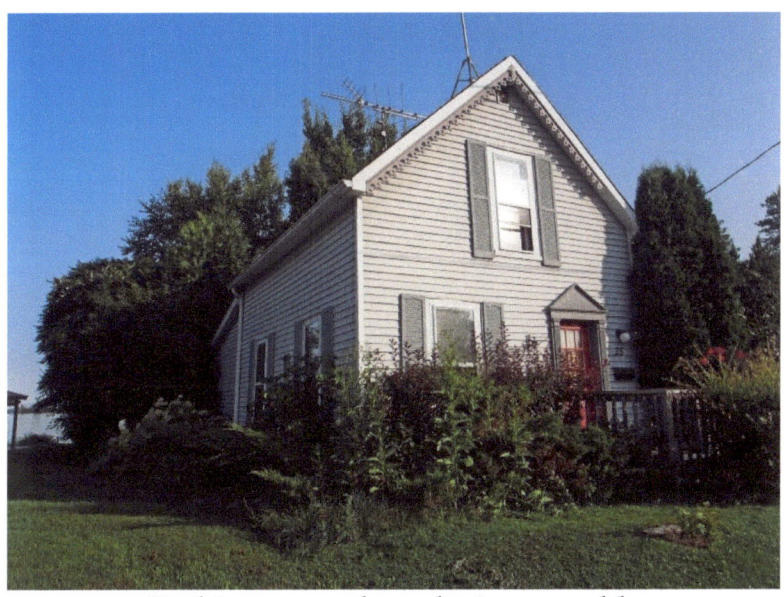

Gothic – verge board trim on gable

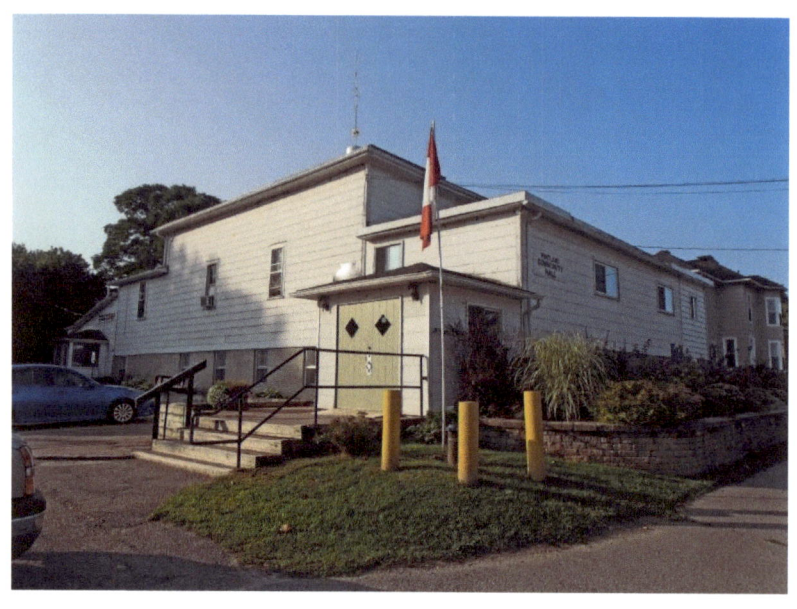

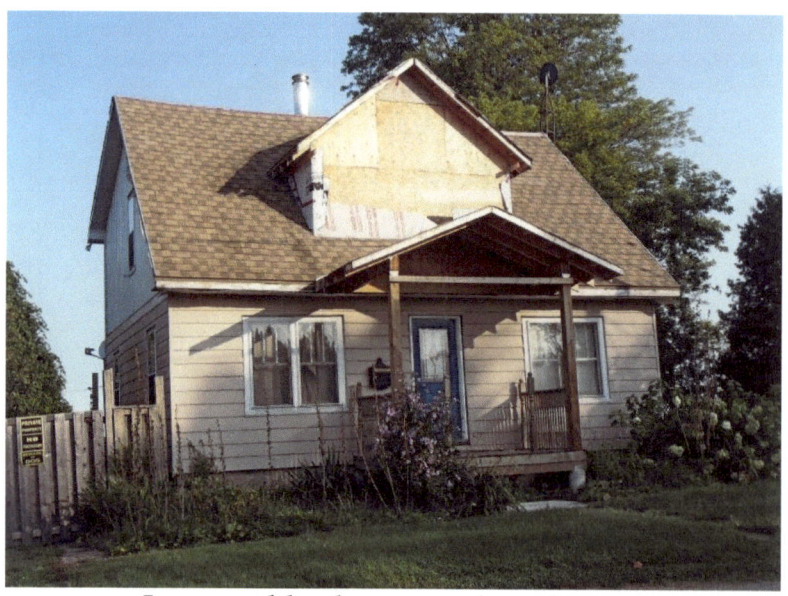

Large gable above porch pediment

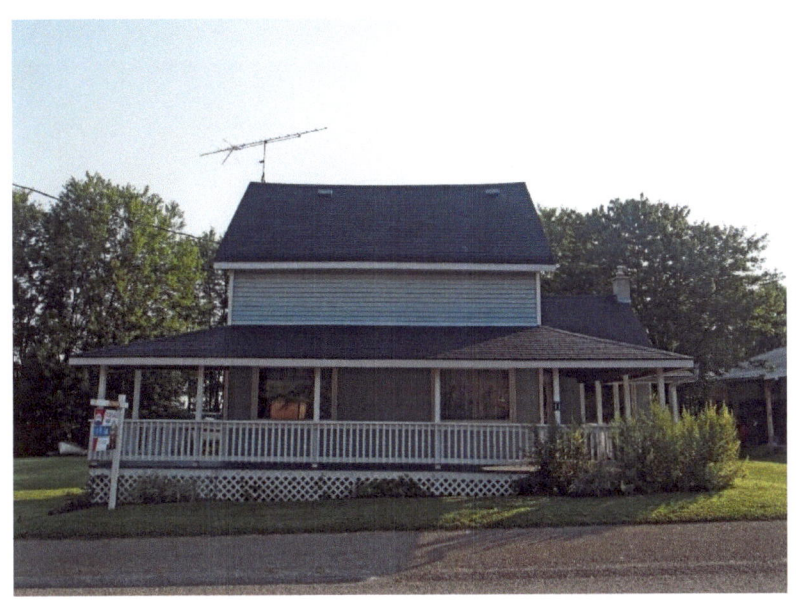

Wraparound veranda

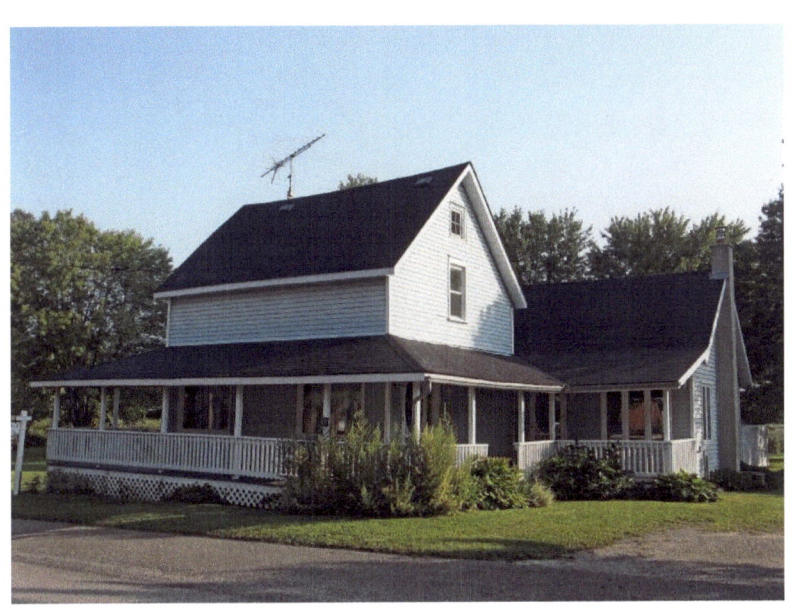

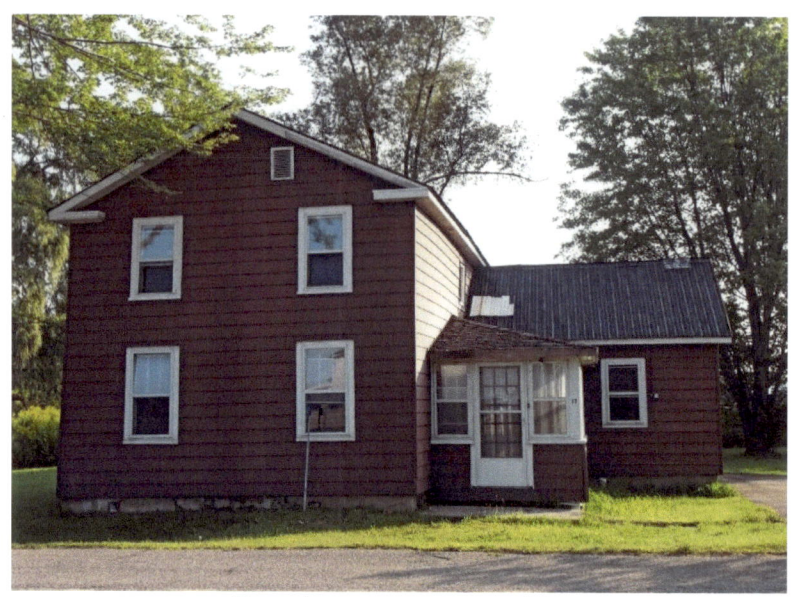

Cornice return on gable

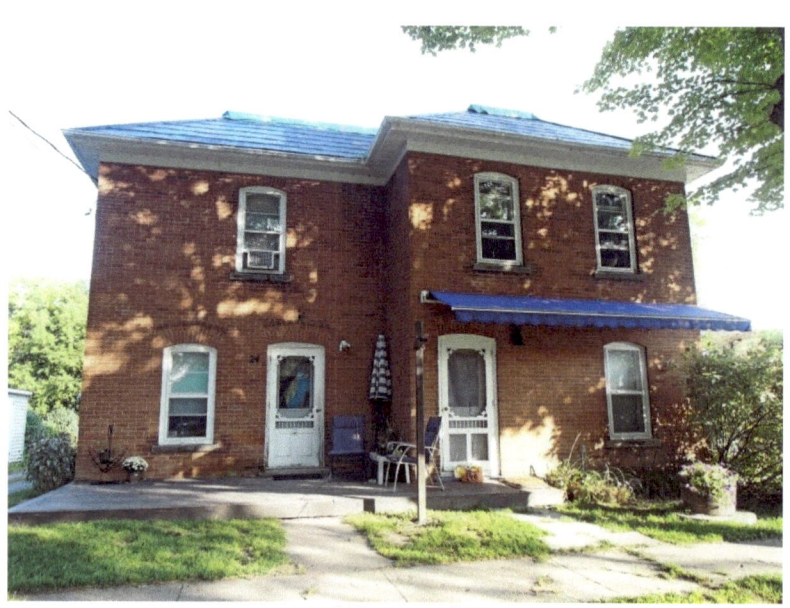

Hip roof

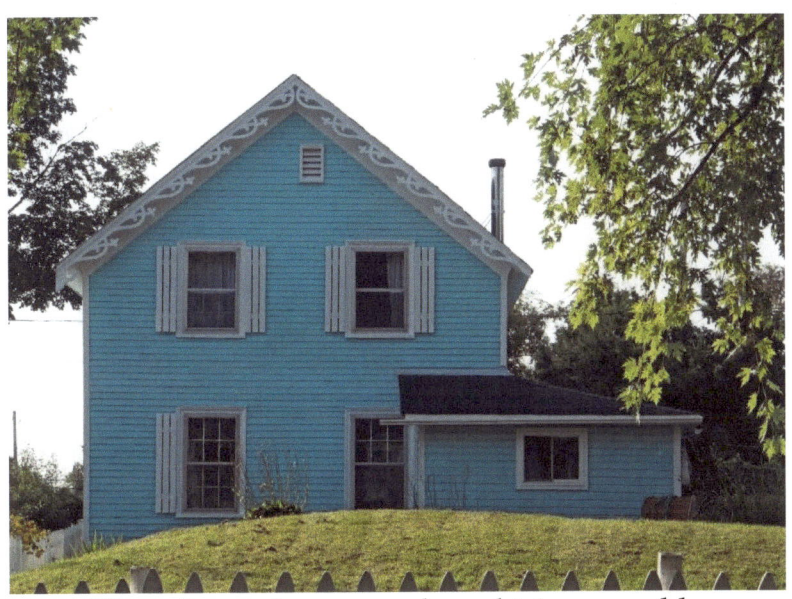

Victorian style – verge board trim on gable

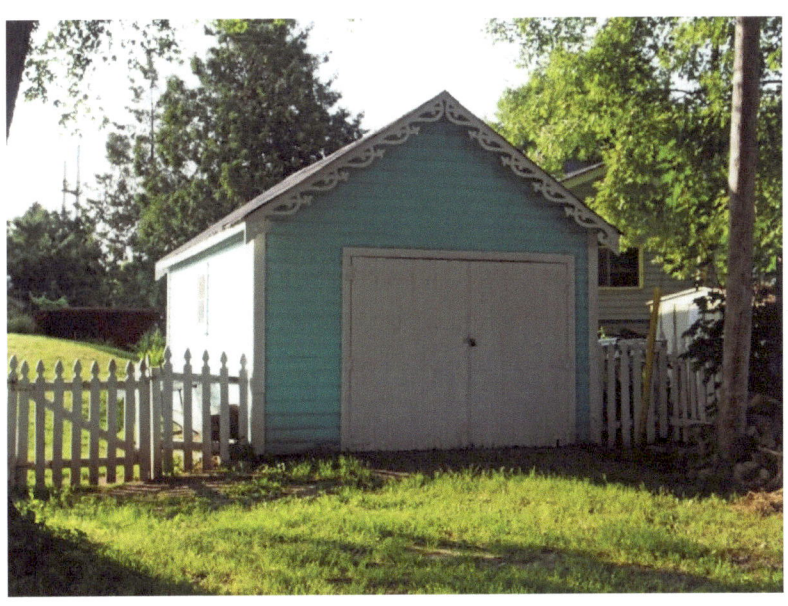

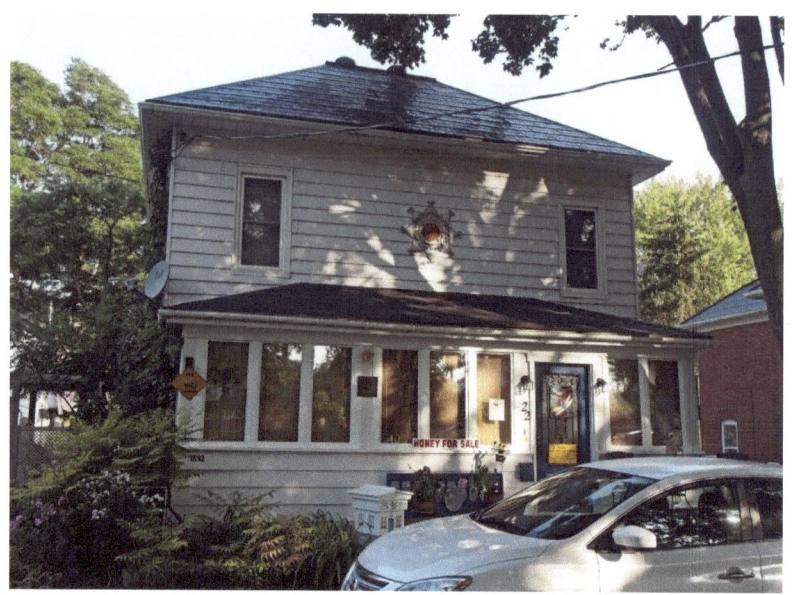

Hip roof, enclosed front porch

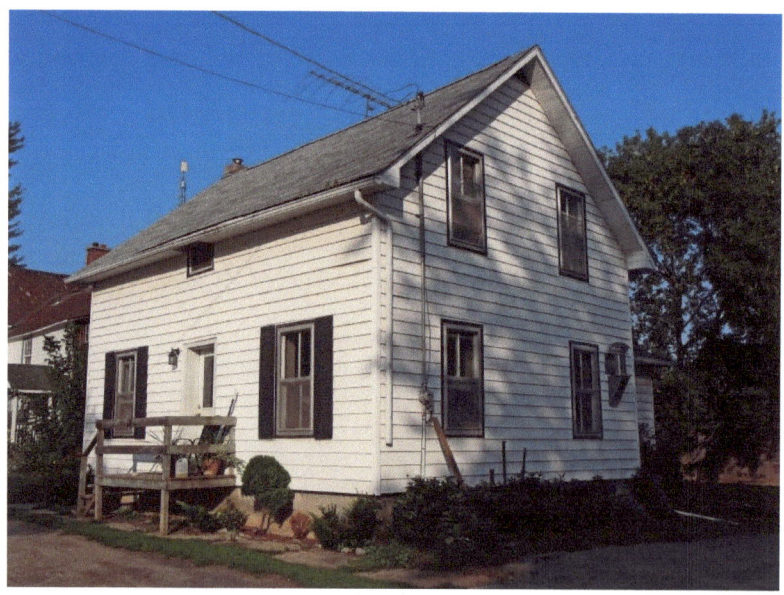

Gothic

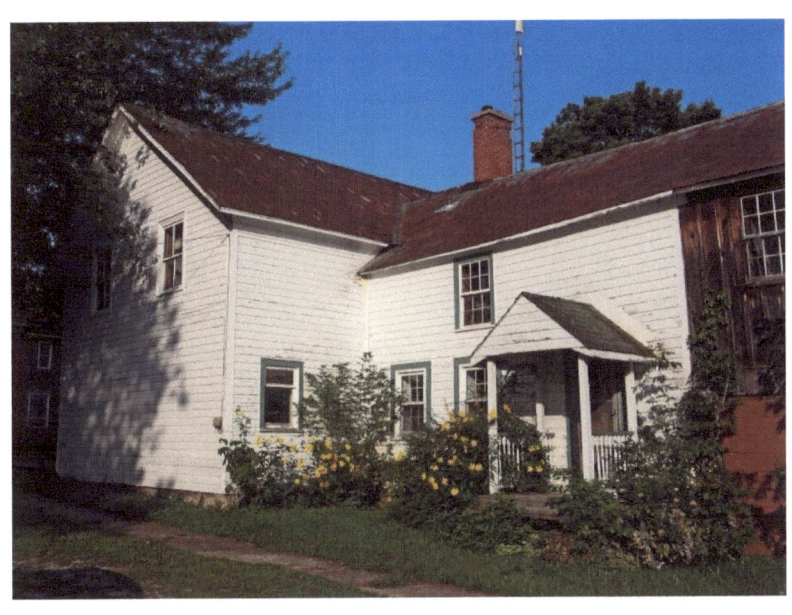

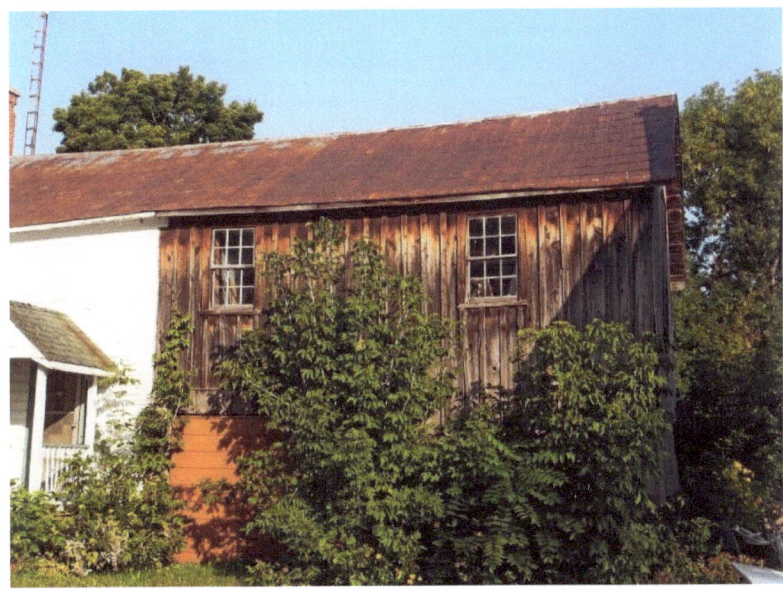

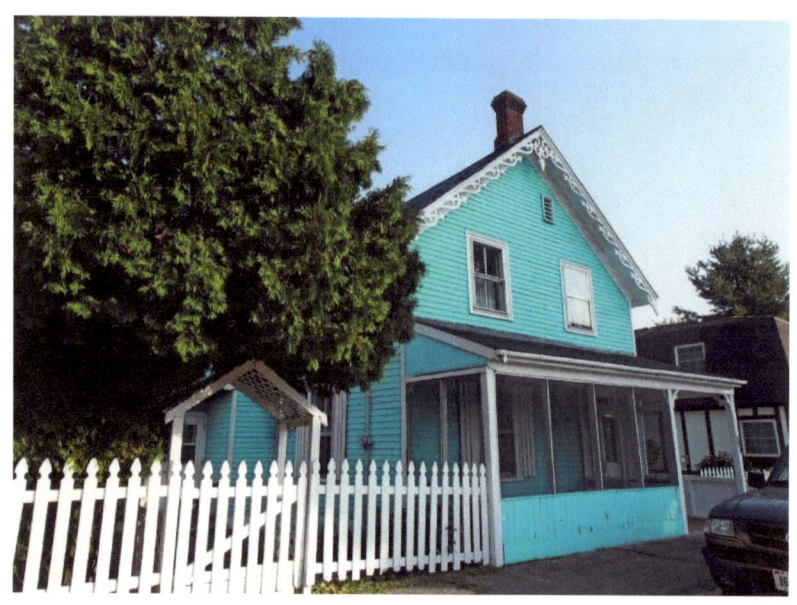

35 Colborne Street – The Gingerbread House – c. 1880s-1890s – Gothic Revival - gingerbread trim with finial on the front gable

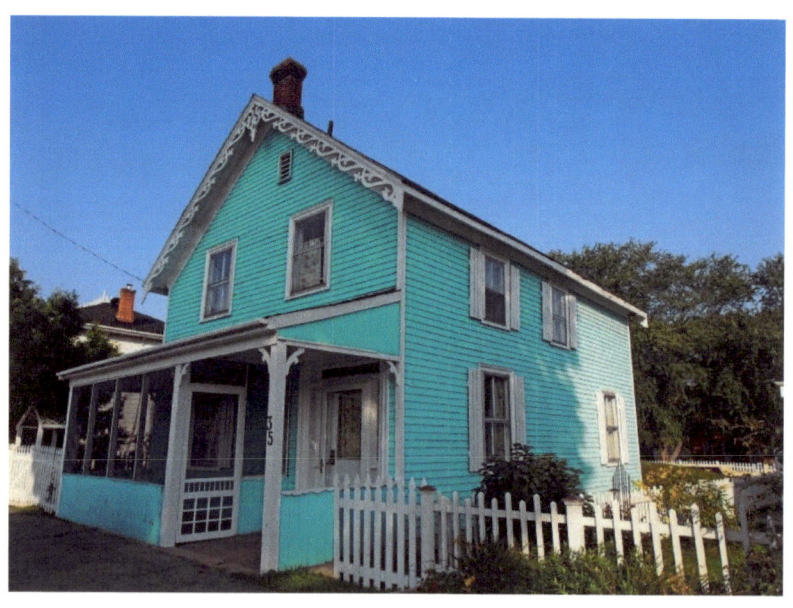

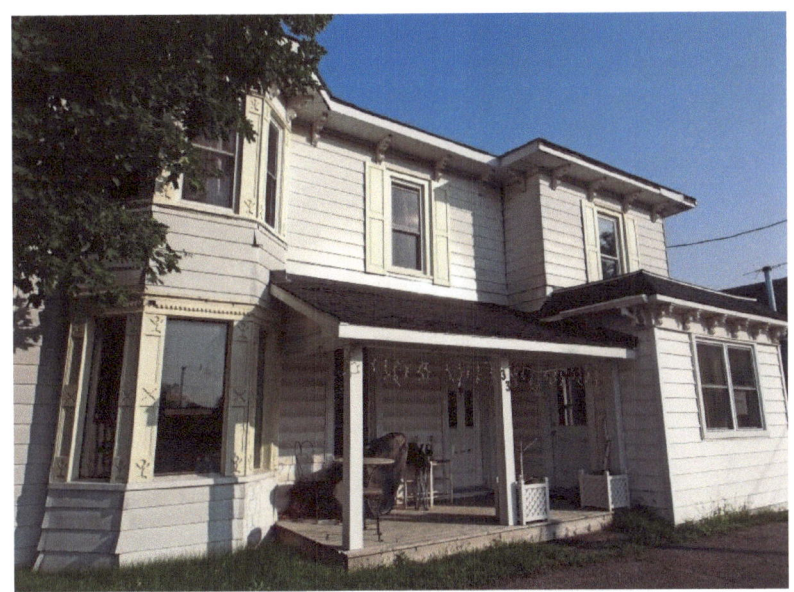

Two-storey bay window, cornice brackets

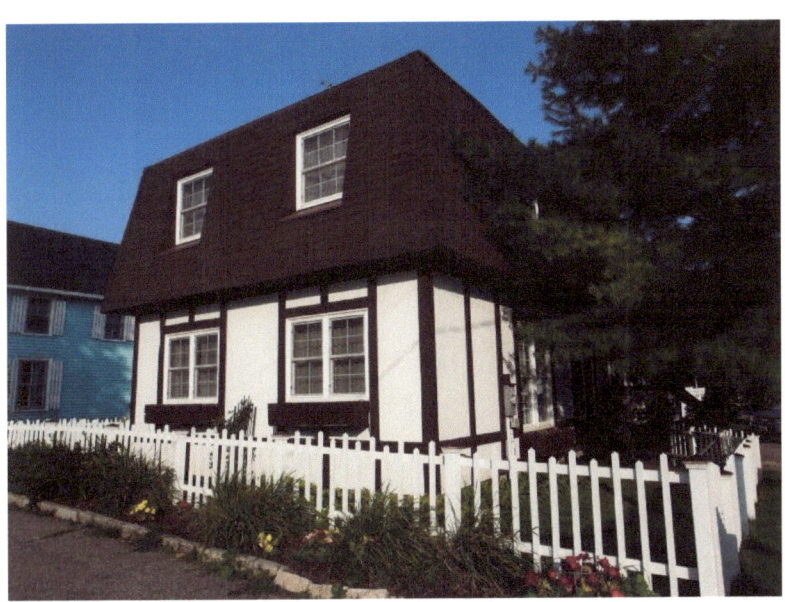

Mansard roof

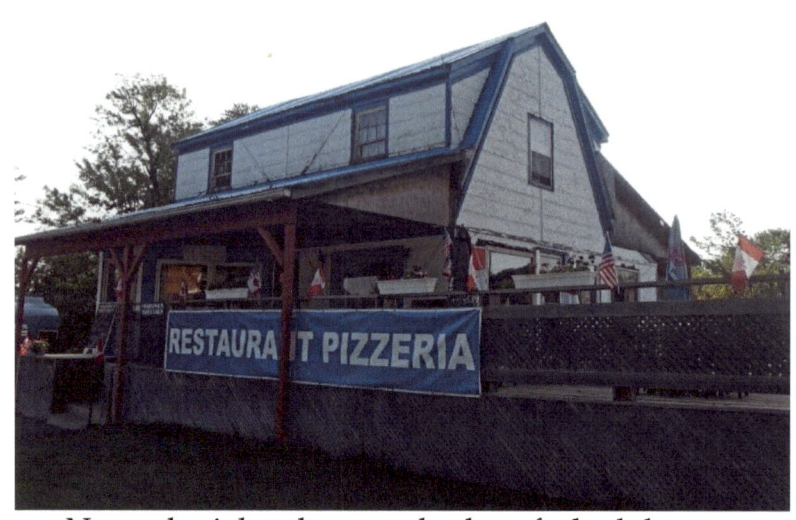

Neo-colonial style – gambrel roof, shed dormer

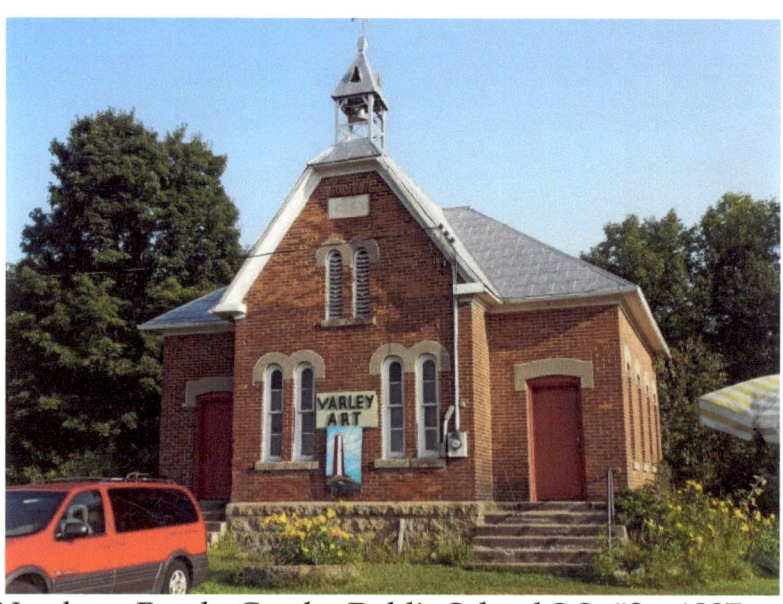

12 Newboro Road - Crosby Public School S.S. #2 – 1907 - now the site of Grace Varley's Art Gallery; separate entrances for boys and girls, tin roof, bell tower, voussoirs

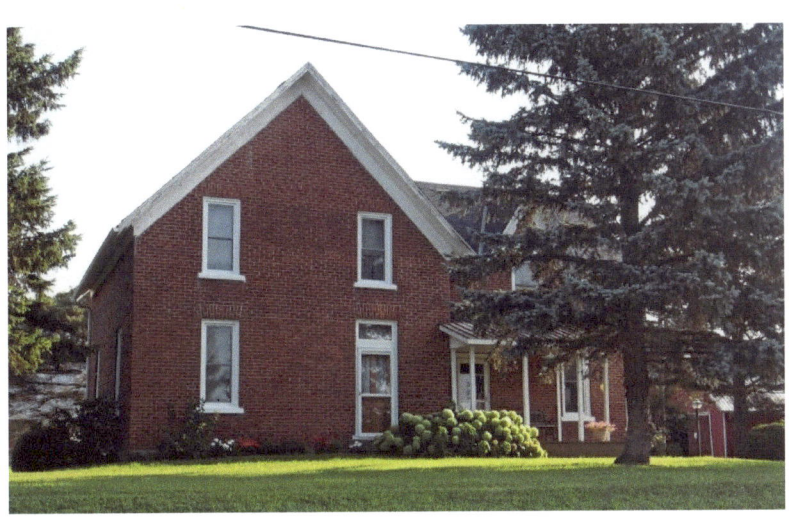

Victorian style

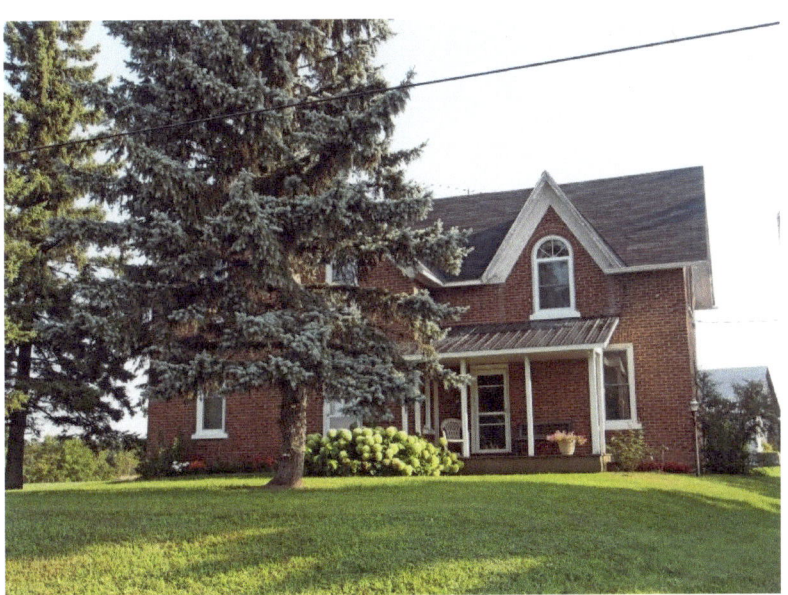

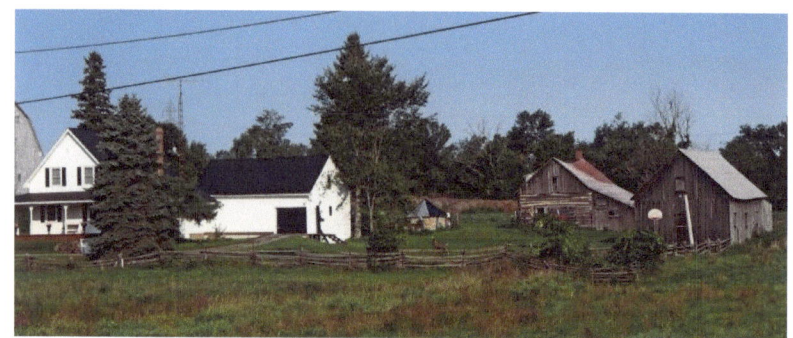

Farm

Newboro

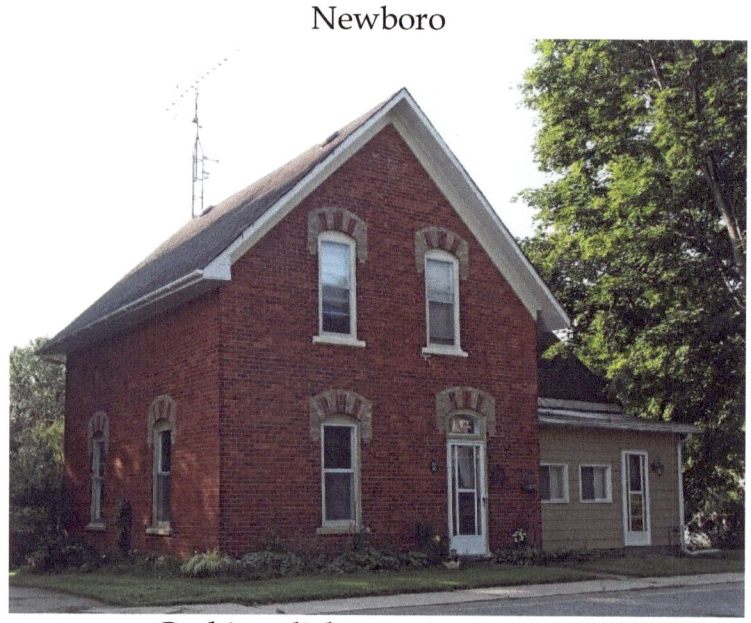

Gothic – dichromatic voussoirs

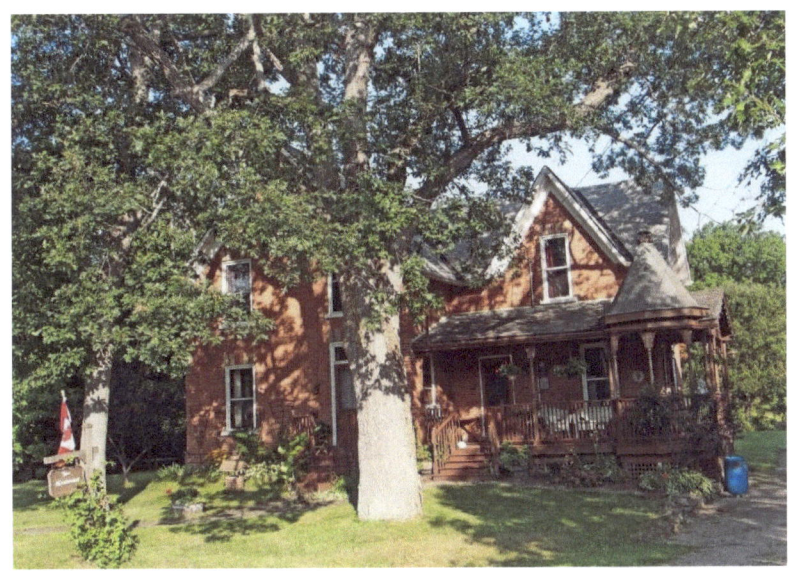

Victorian

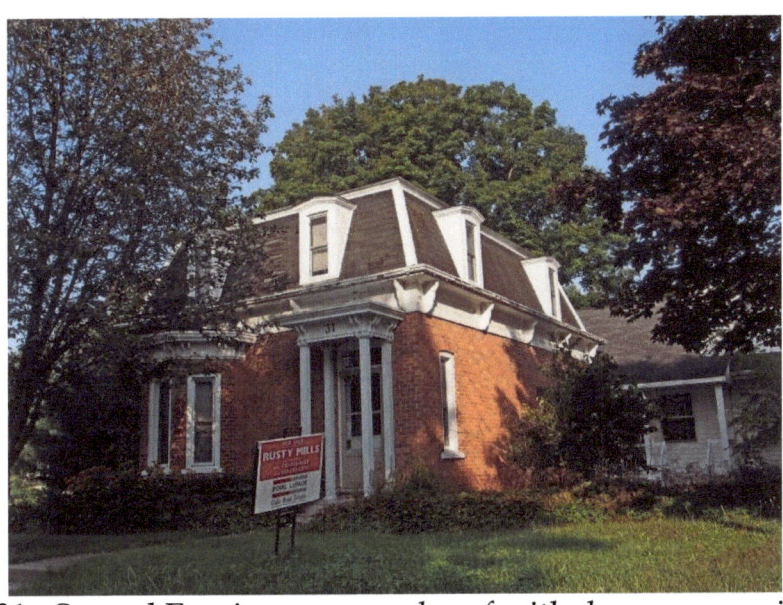

#31 - Second Empire – mansard roof with dormers, cornice brackets, bay window

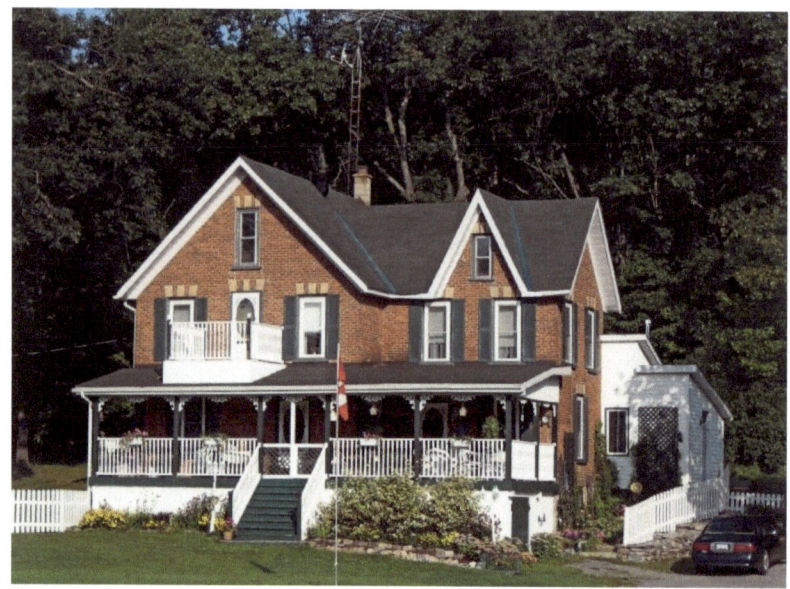

Victorian - dichromatic voussoirs, verandah pillars with ornate capitals, open railing

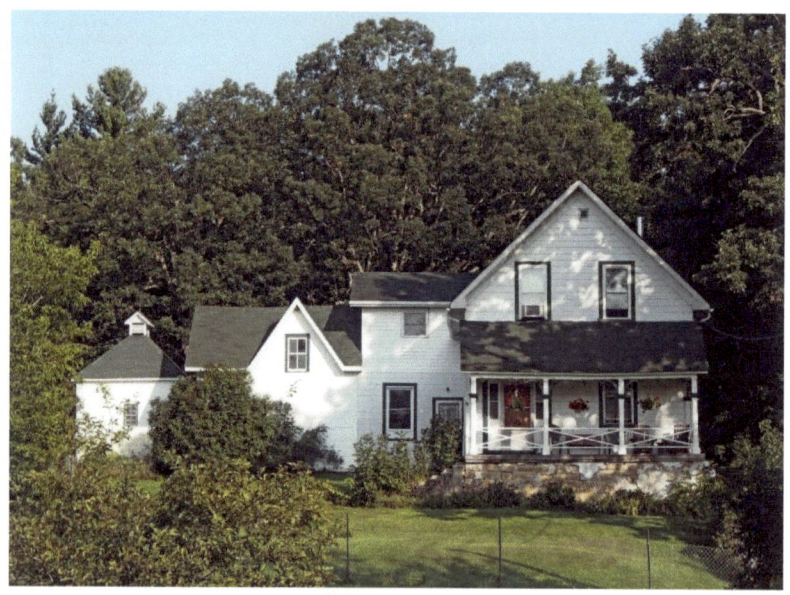

Victorian

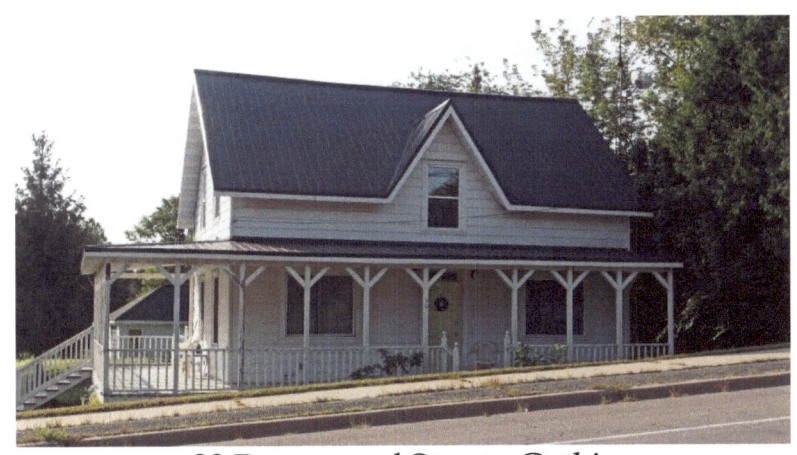

30 Drummond Street - Gothic

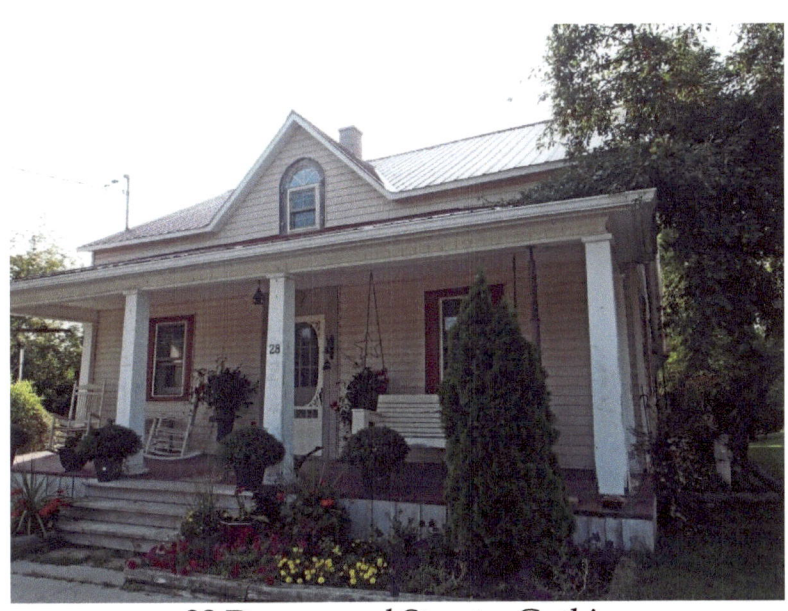

28 Drummond Street – Gothic

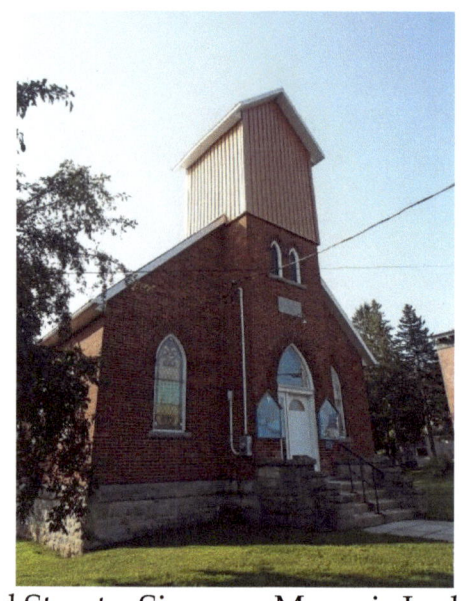

26 Drummond Street – Simpson Masonic Lodge, Newboro -
lancet windows

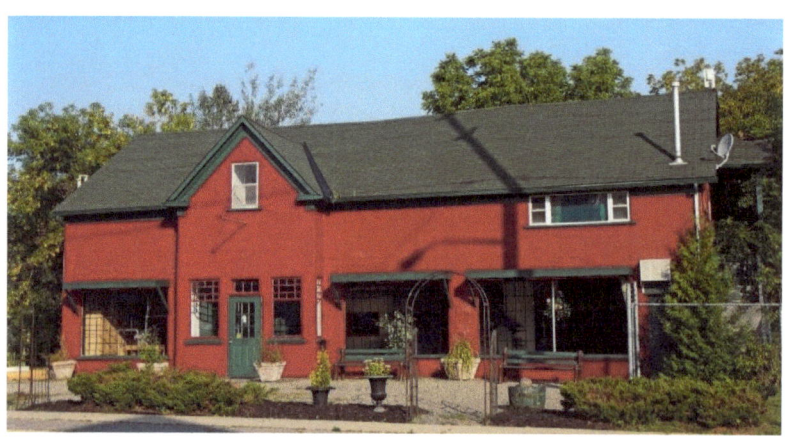

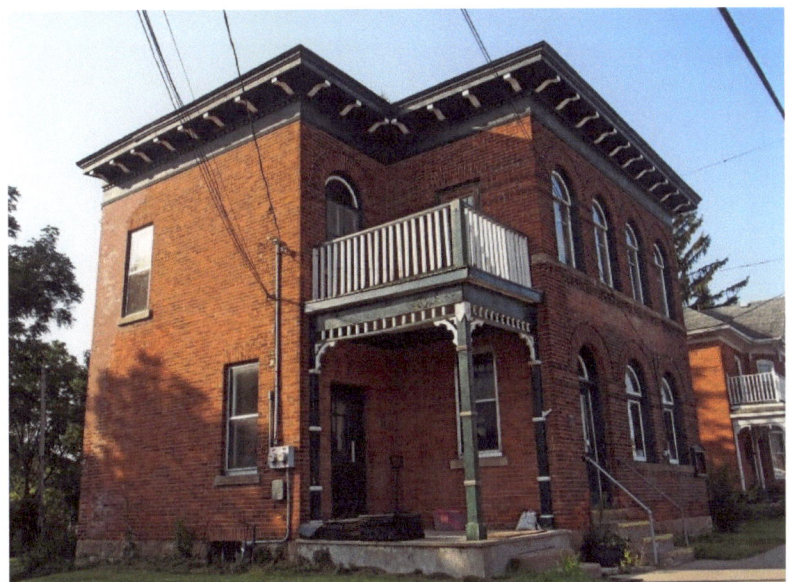

24 Drummond Street – Italianate – Union Bank Building – cornice brackets, second floor balcony, voussoirs, string course

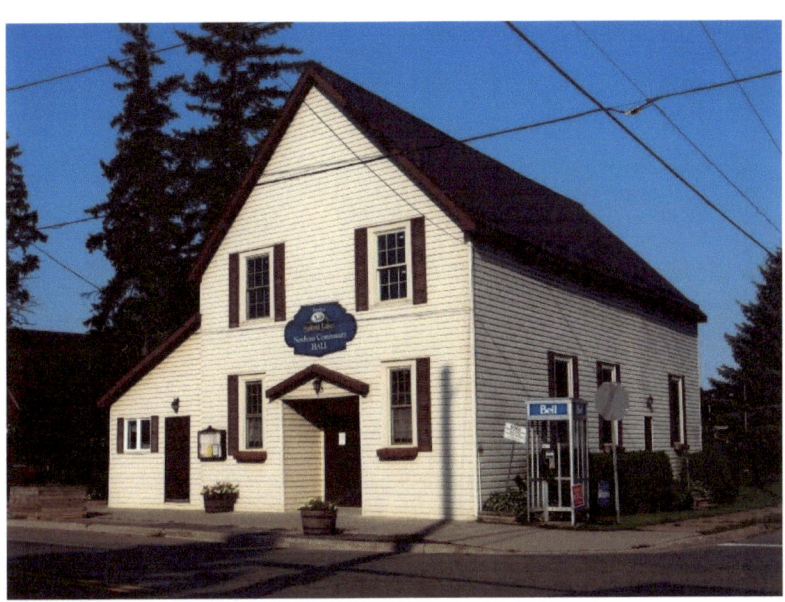

15 Drummond Street - Newboro Community Hall - Gothic

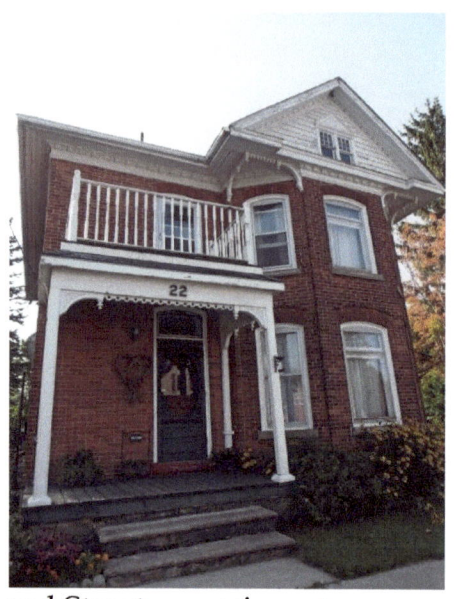

22 Drummond Street – cornice return on gable, dentil molding, fretwork, second floor balcony

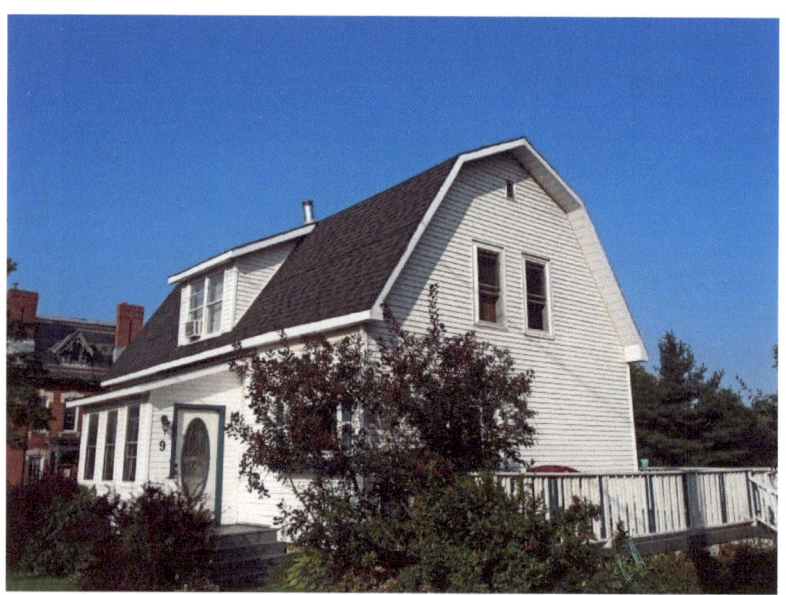

9 Drummond Street – Neo-colonial – gambrel roof, dormer

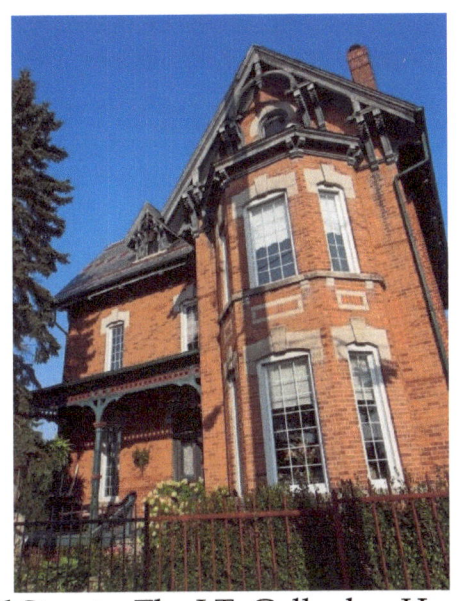

7 Drummond Street – The J.T. Gallagher House – c. 1885 –
Gothic Revival style – 2½ storeys tall, 2 storey bay, extensive
dripped barge board, locally quarried sandstone lintels; ornate
polychromatic slate roof; tall decorative chimneys

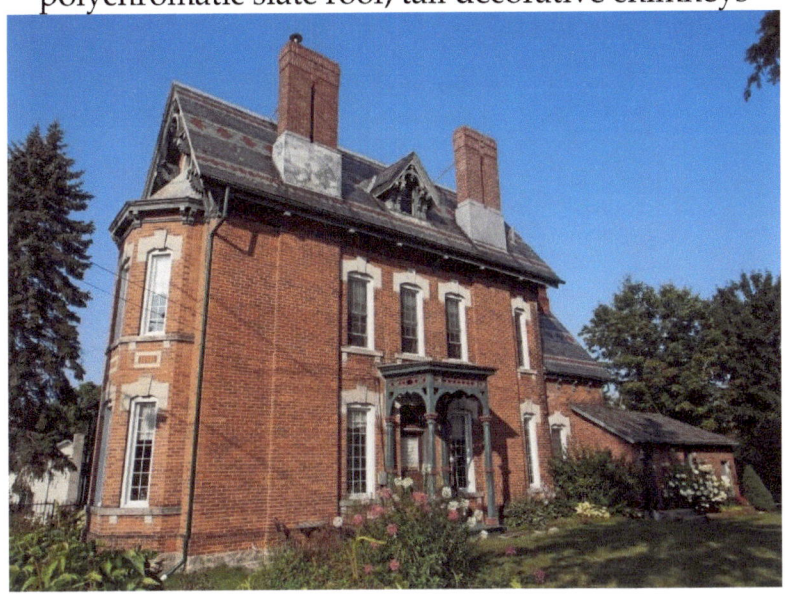

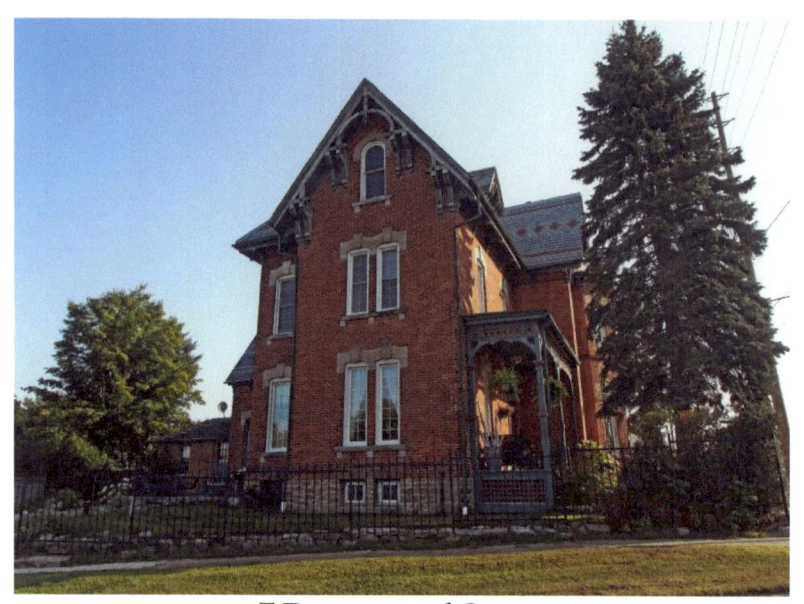

7 Drummond Street

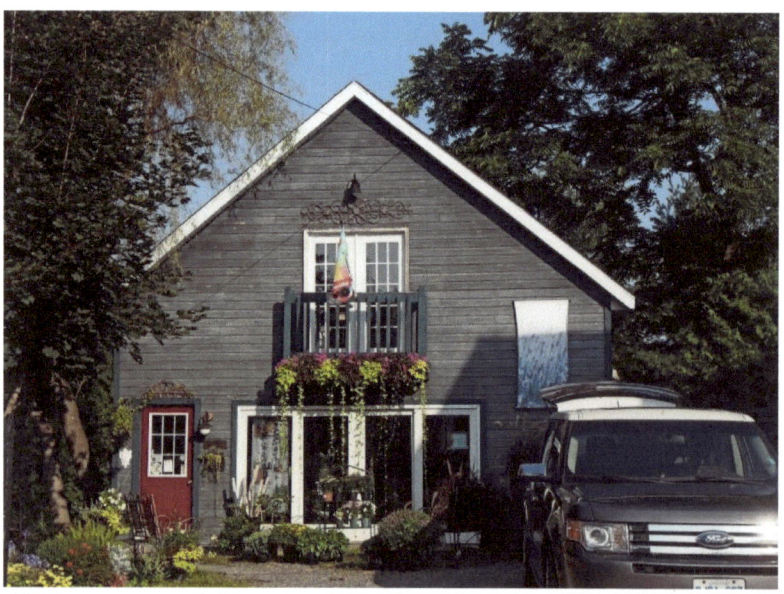

7 Drummond Street – Hidden Garden Floral Designs

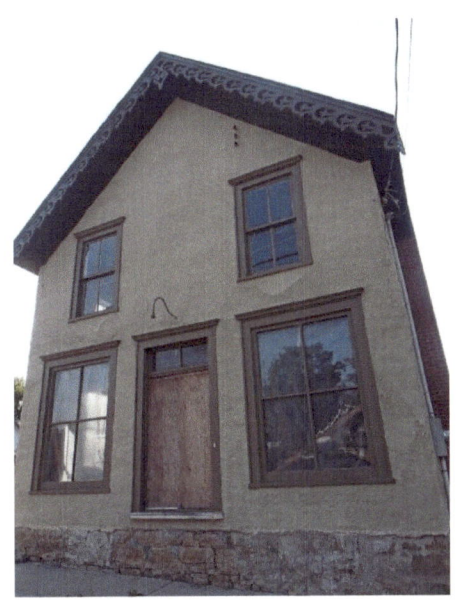

Gothic – verge board trim on gable

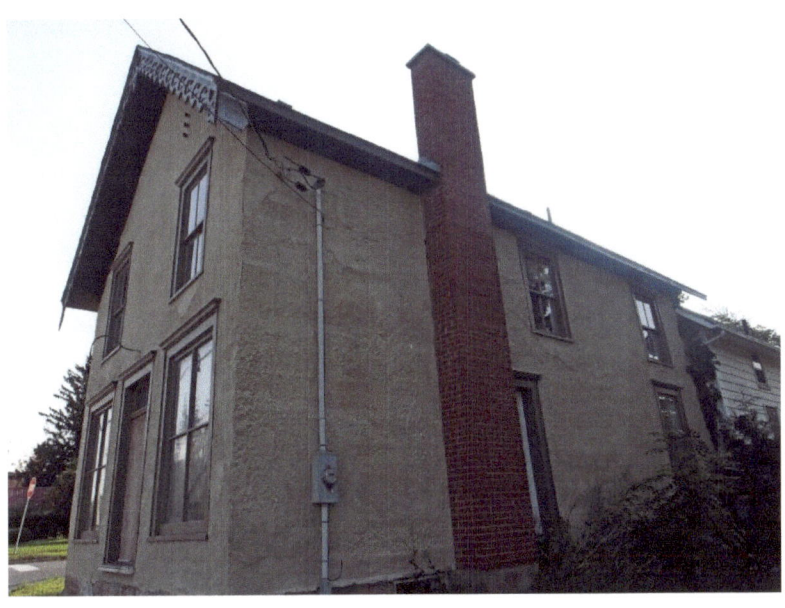

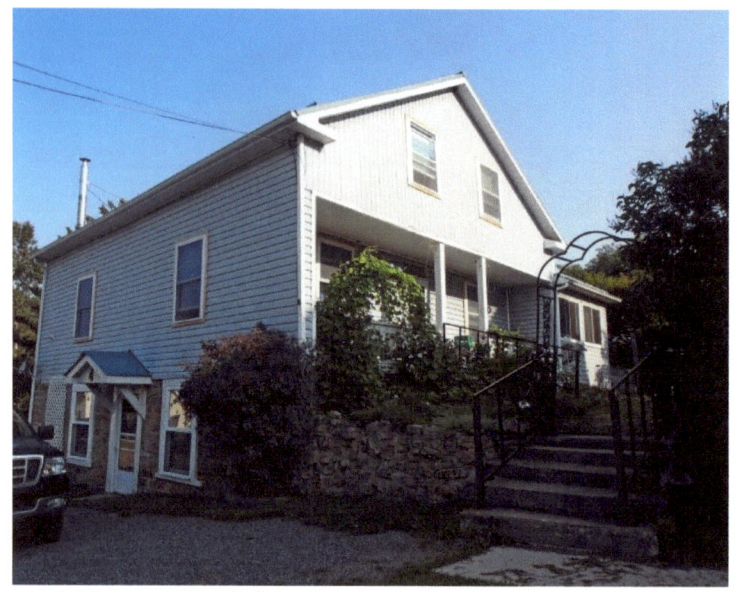

4 Drummond Street - cornice return on gable

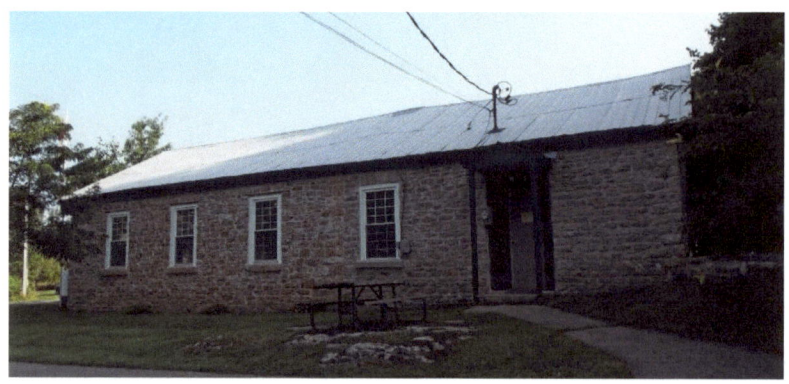

10 Brock Street – The Court House - 1840

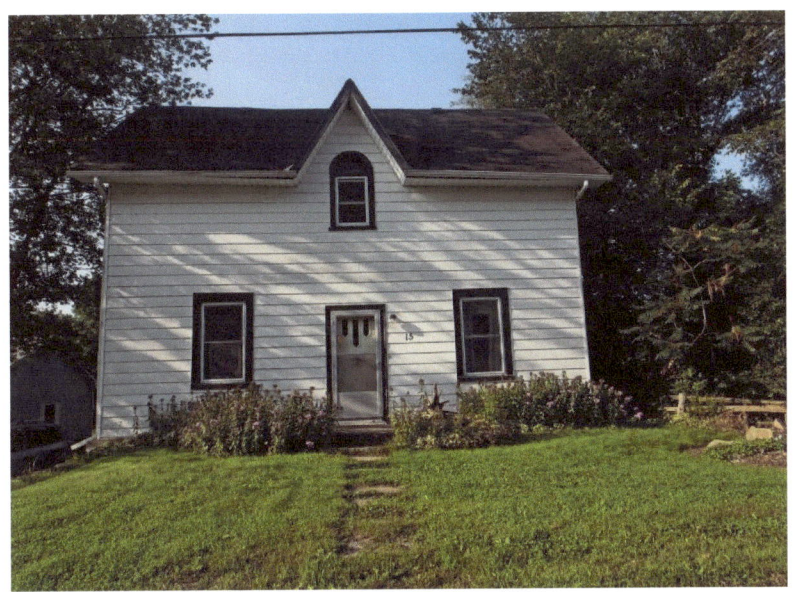

#15 – Gothic Cottage

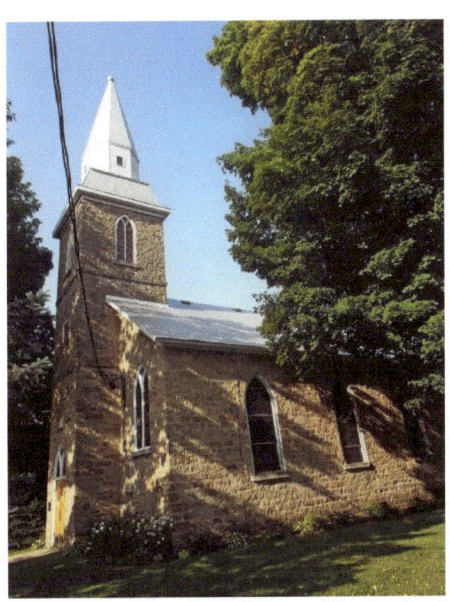

15 Brock Street - St. Mary's Anglican Church, Newboro – 1850
– Gothic Revival style, high walls, belfry with a short spire on
a square tower; stained glass windows; lancet windows

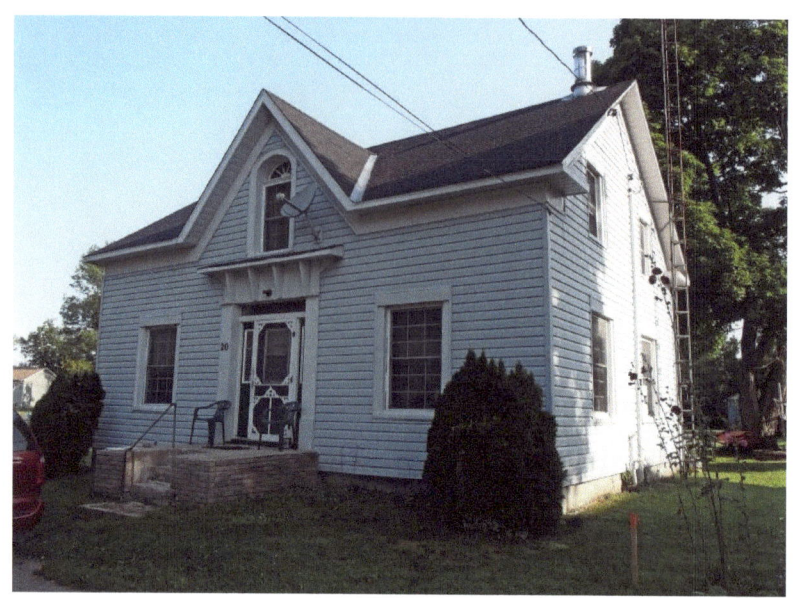

#20 – Gothic Cottage

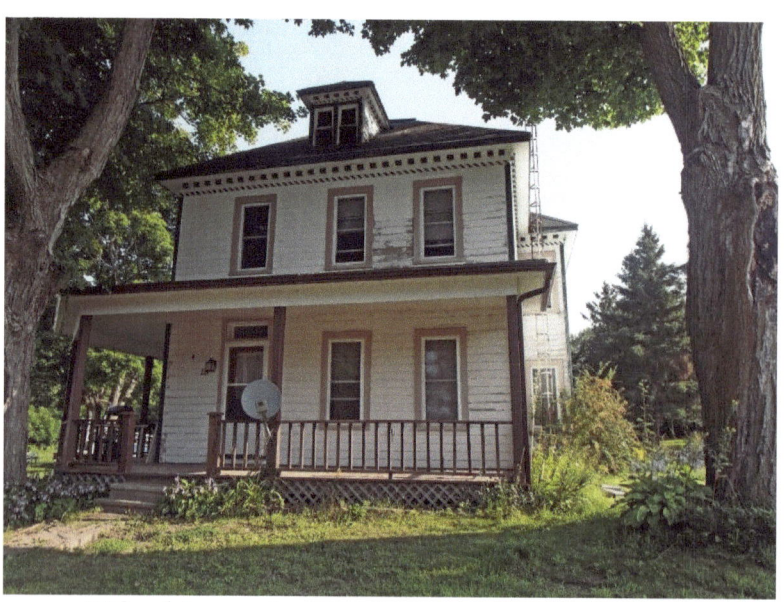

#18 – hip roof with dormer, dentil molding

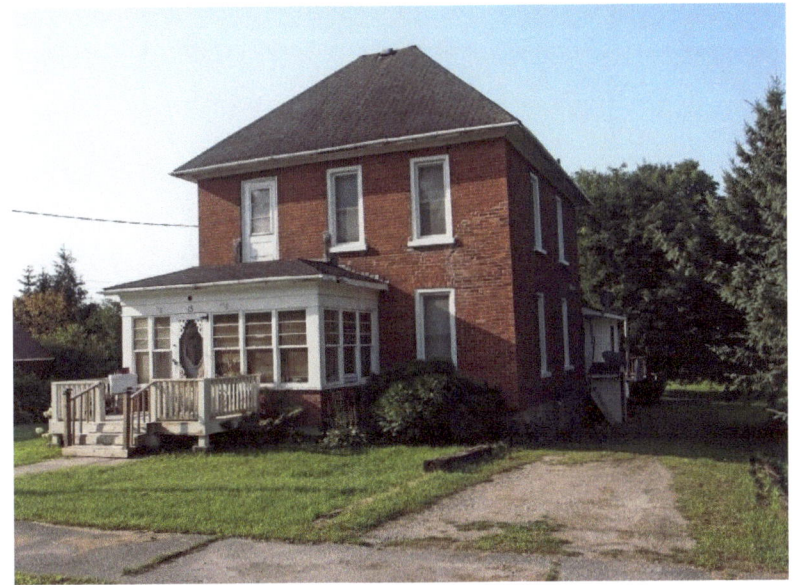

#15 – hipped roof

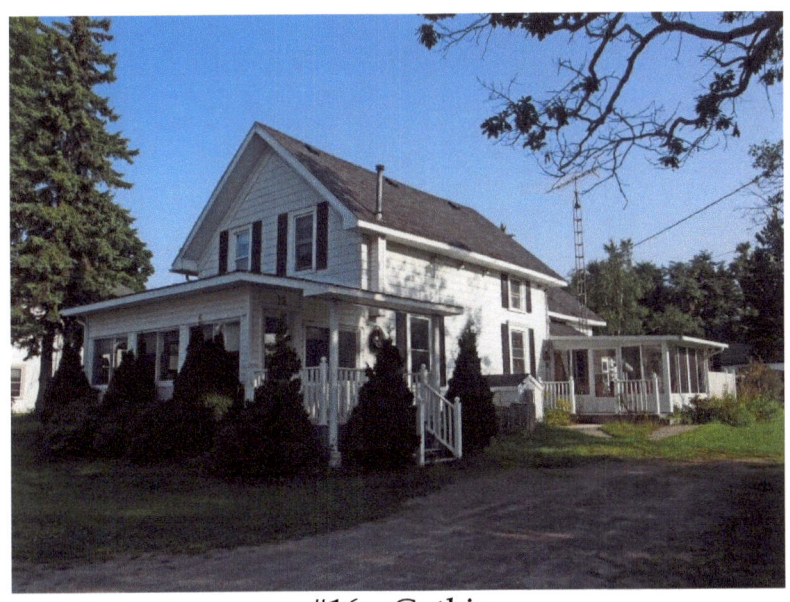

#16 – Gothic

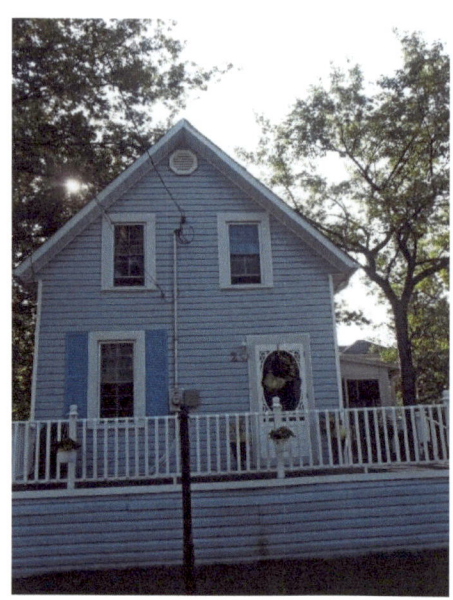

#2

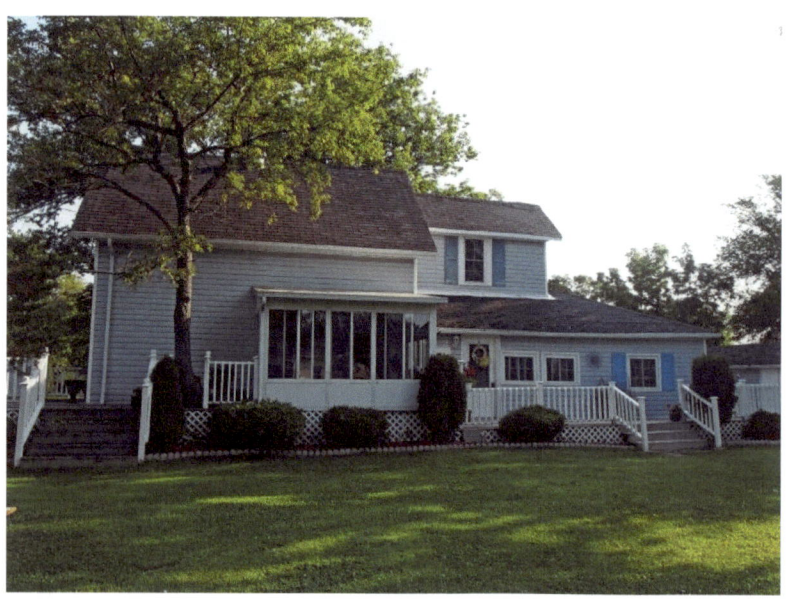

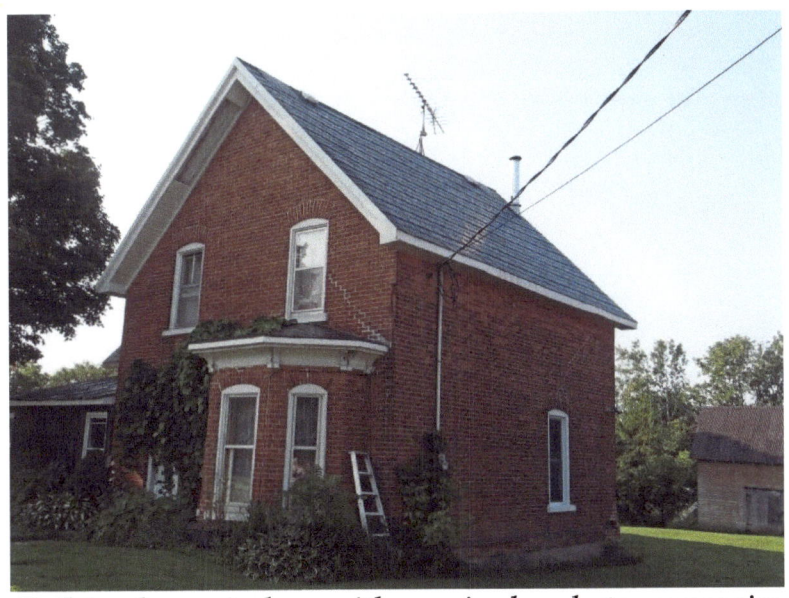

Gothic – bay window with cornice brackets; voussoirs

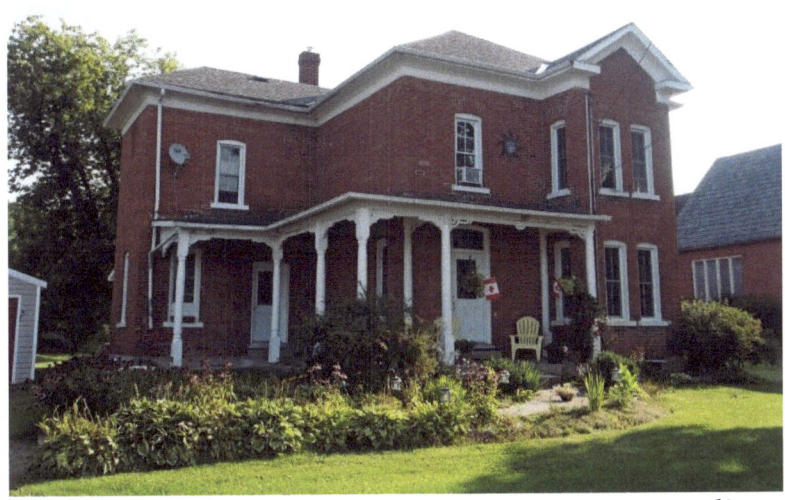

Italianate – hipped roof, cornice return on open pediment above two-storey tower-like bay; voussoirs over windows; veranda pillars with decorative capitals

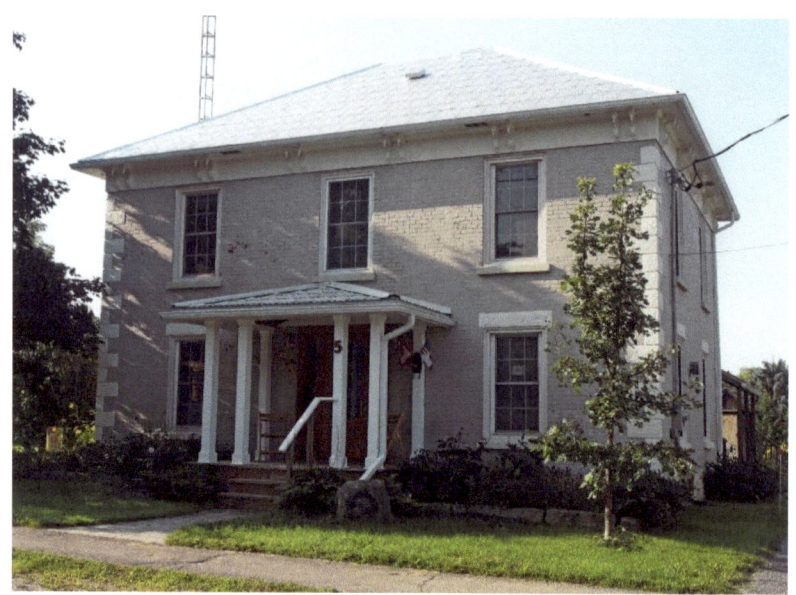

#5 – hip roof, paired cornice brackets, corner quoins

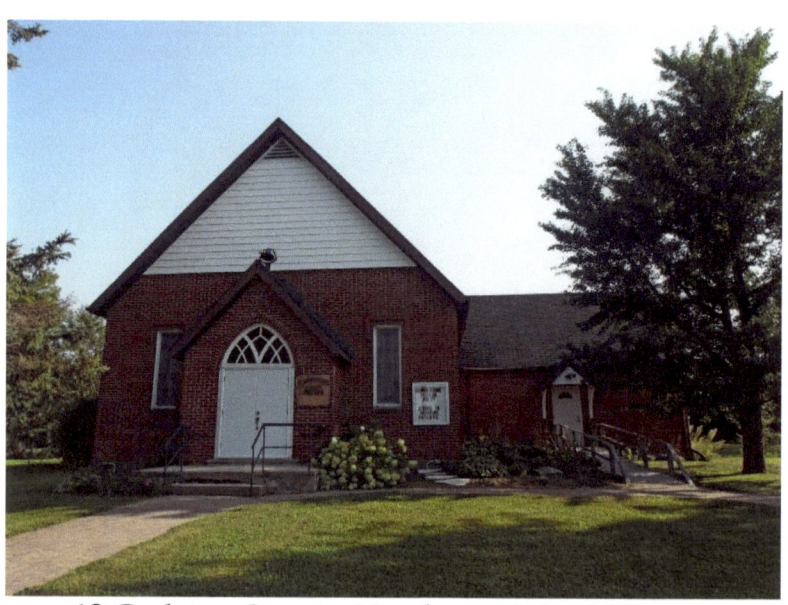

12 Carleton Street - Newboro United Church

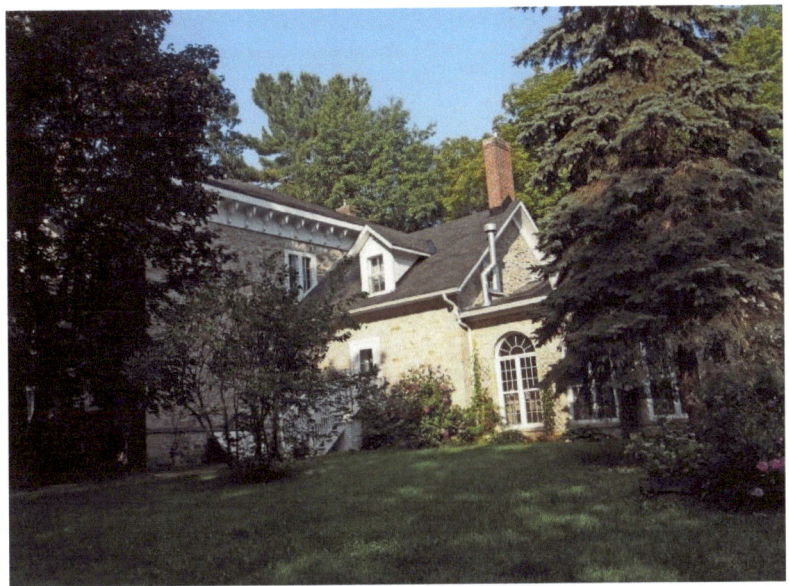

Cobblestone architecture – two-storey section with cornice brackets; one-storey gabled wing with dormer

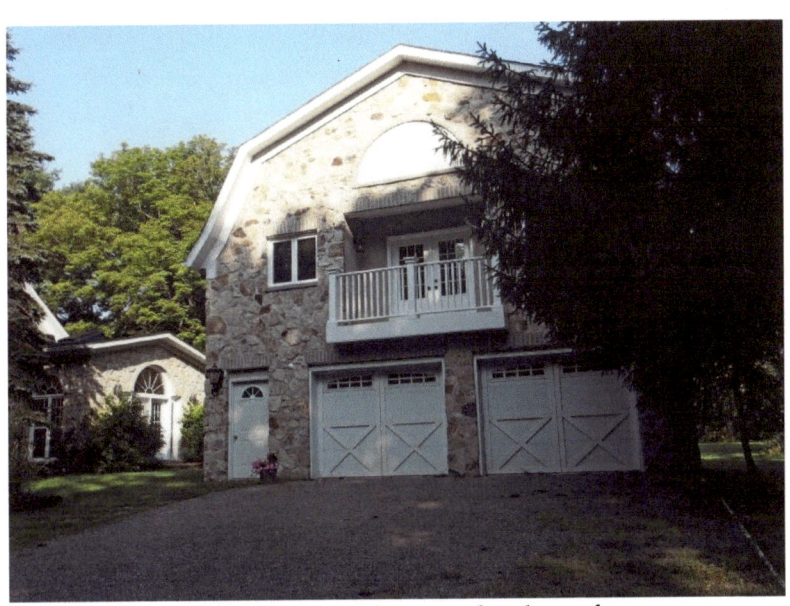

Neo-colonial – gambrel roof

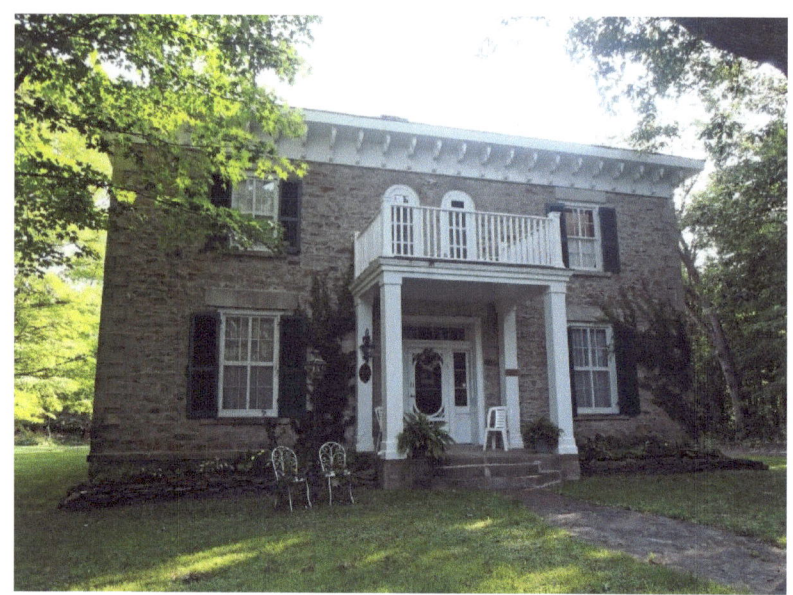

#11 New Street – The John Draffin House – c. 1860 – first stone building constructed in Newboro – Italianate – corner quoins with large ashlars; cornice brackets, two round-headed doors opening onto balcony above porch; sidelights and transom – between 1895 and 1945 this was the parsonage for St. Mary's Church

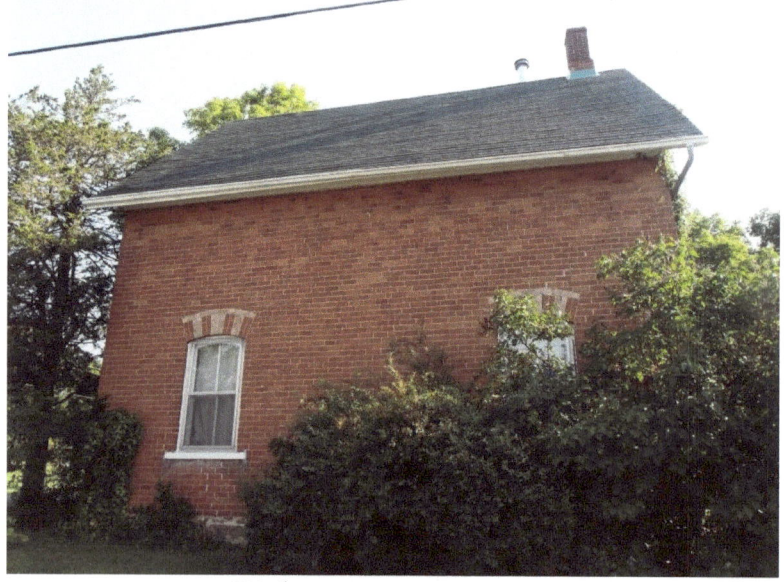

Dichromatic voussoirs

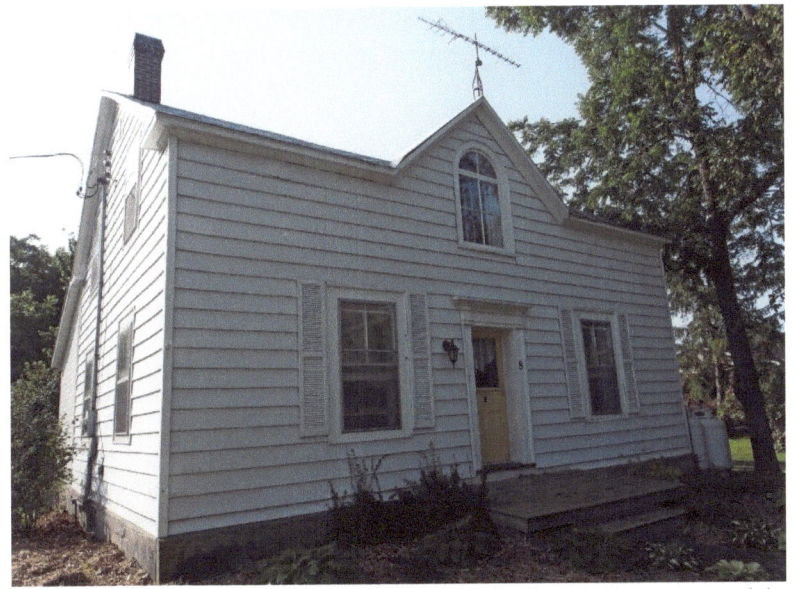

#8 – Ontario Cottage - round-headed window in gable

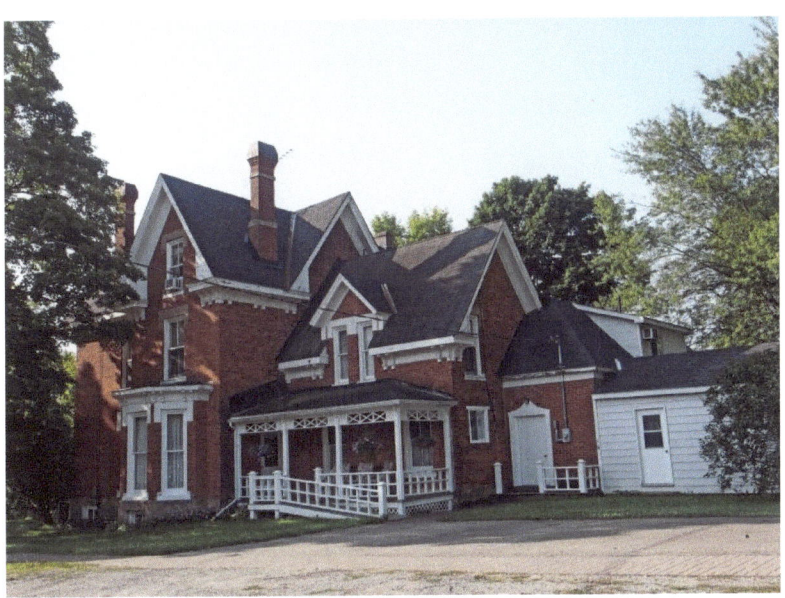

14 By Street – The John Poole Tett House – c. 1896 – Victorian – tall, imposing windows; bay window; cornice brackets

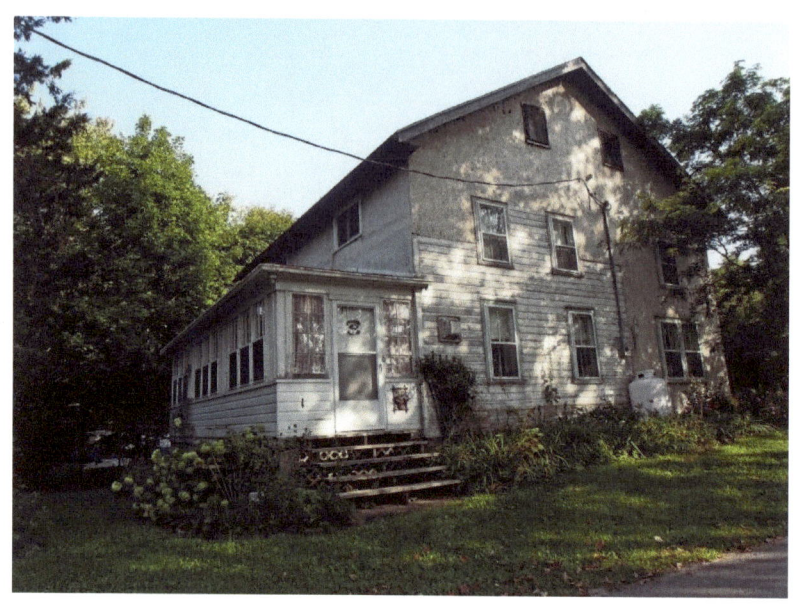

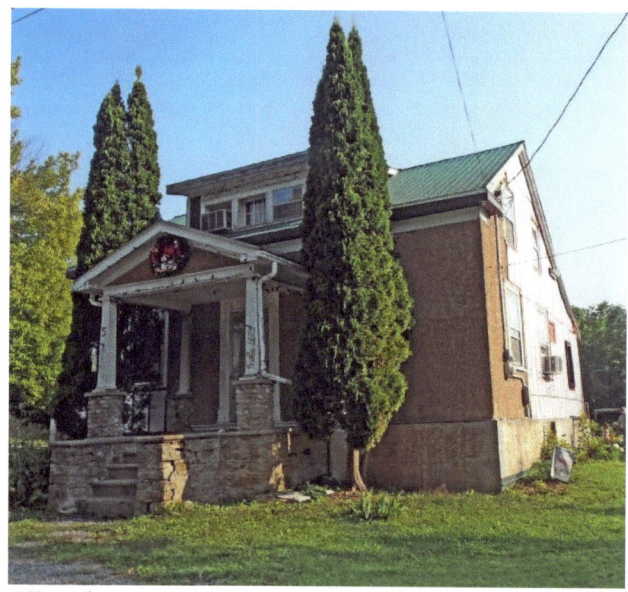

#5 – dormer in attic, pediment above porch

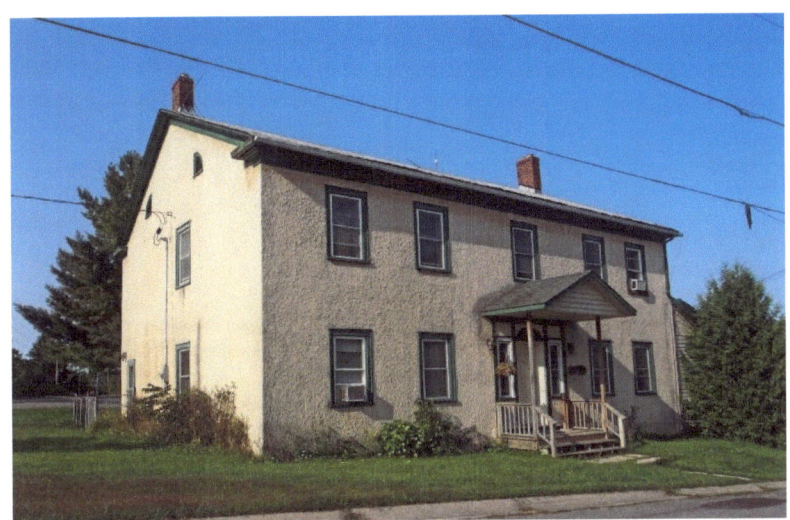

Georgian – balanced façade, cornice return on end gable

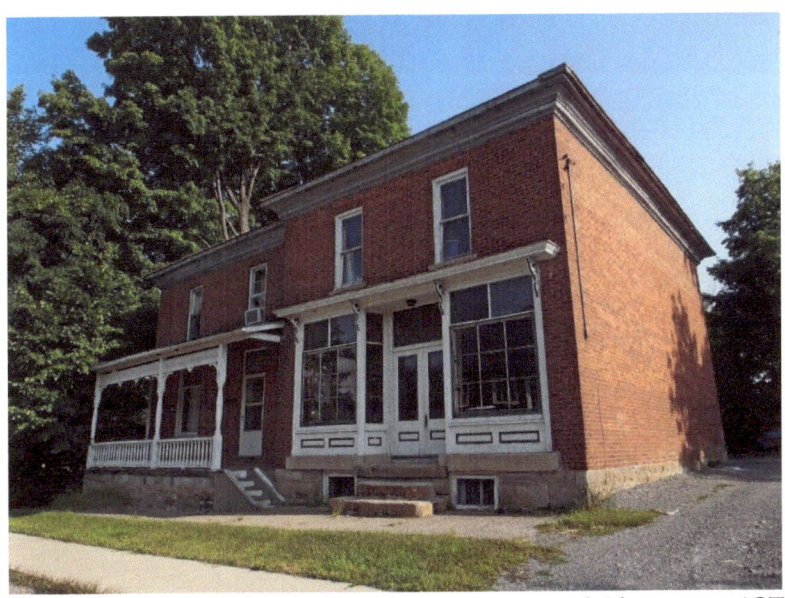

4 Main Street – The R.O. Leggett House and Shop – c. 1870 – furniture and undertaking establishment – intricate treillage work on the veranda posts of the home; large windows of business

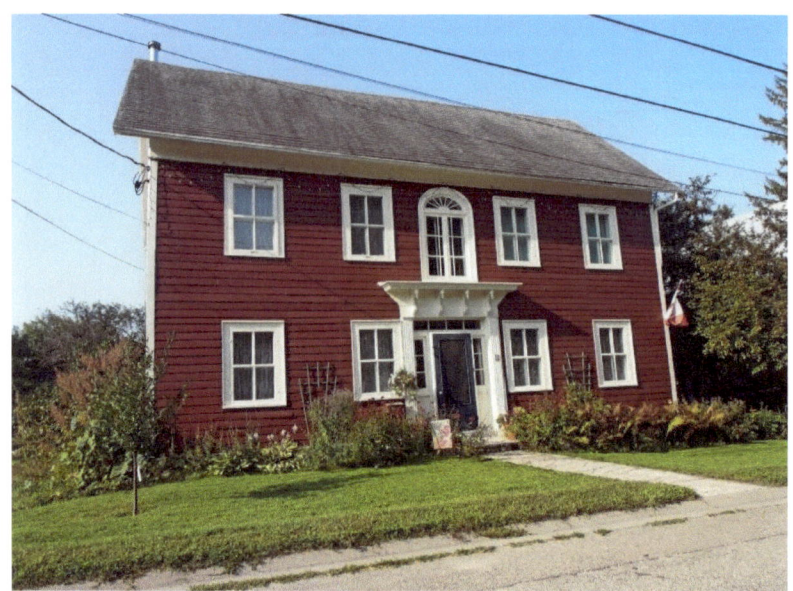

5 Main Street – John Webster House – c. 1860s – Classical Revival style – entrance has a rectangular transom with sidelights to let natural light into the central hallway before there was electricity; bracketed shelf above door; Doric engaged columns flanking the sidelights; central casement window has a fanlight transom above it

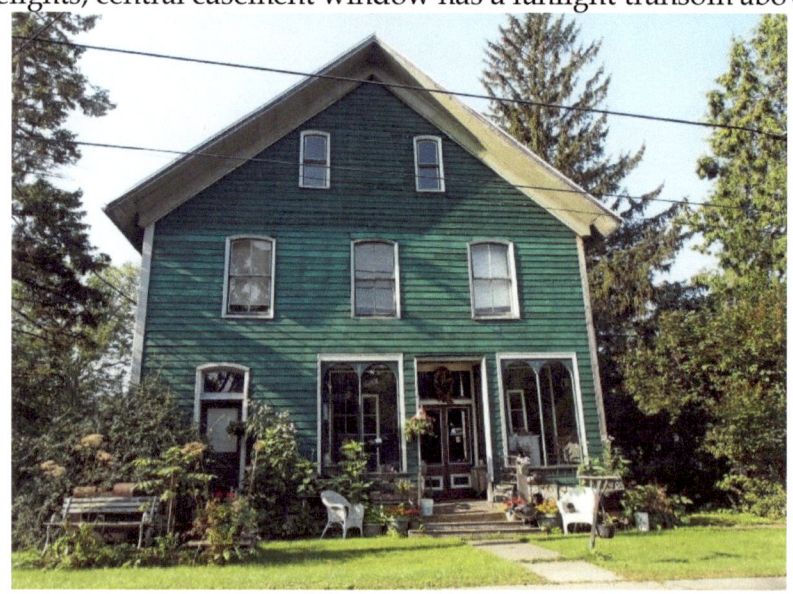

Wood siding

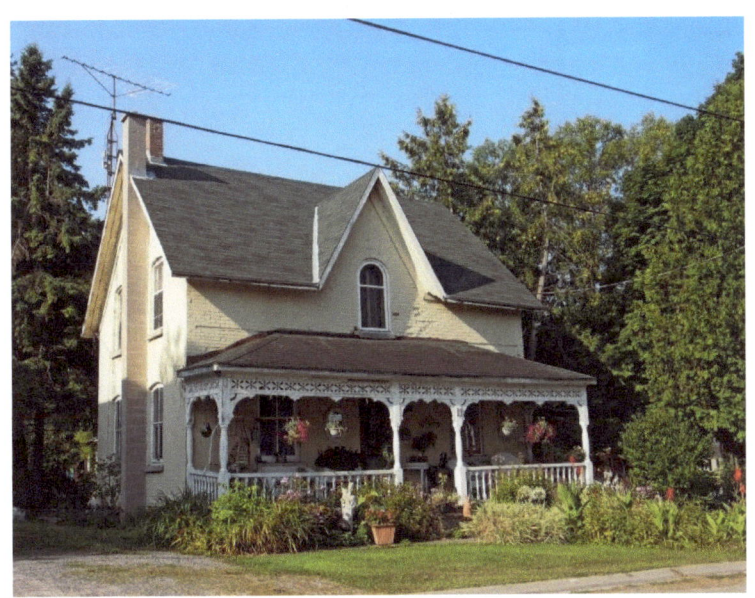

14 Main Street – The Richard Blake House - c. 1858 – Ontario Cottage – 1½ storeys; gable window over front doorway provided light to a central hallway on the upper floor; intricate treillage work on the veranda posts, open railing

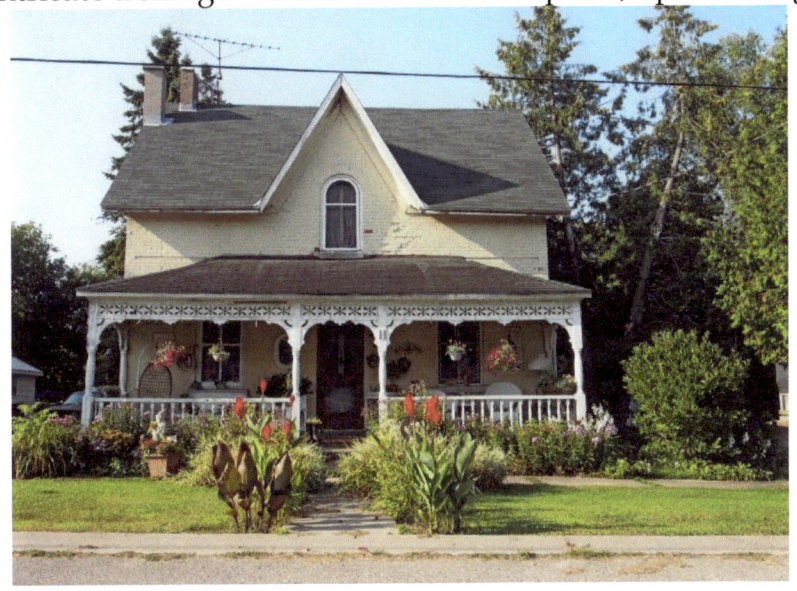

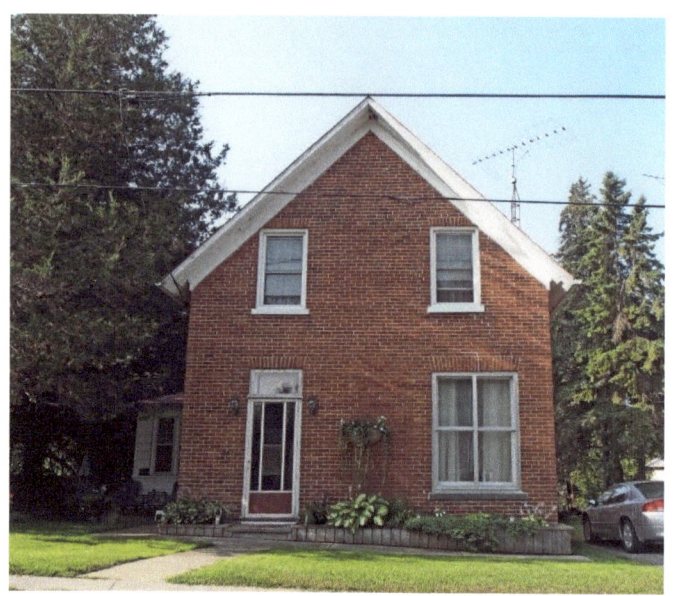

Gothic

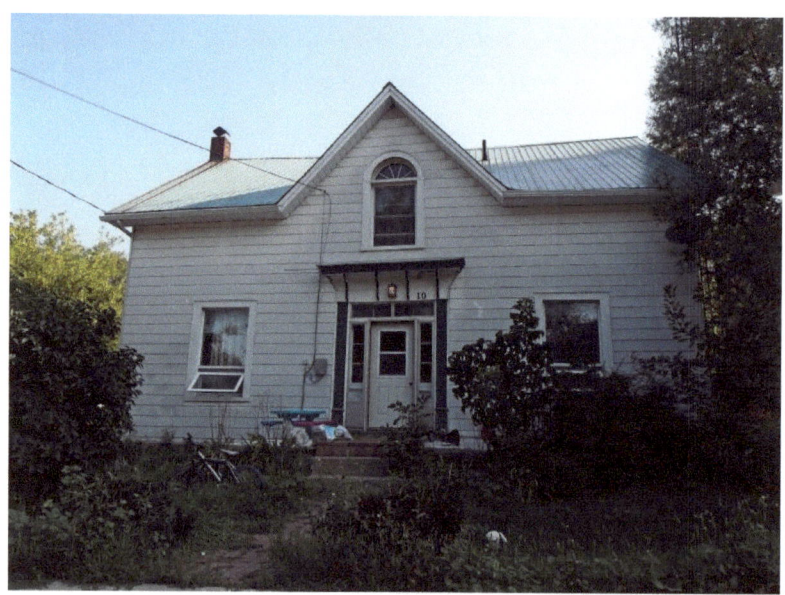

#10 – Ontario Cottage - round-headed window in gable

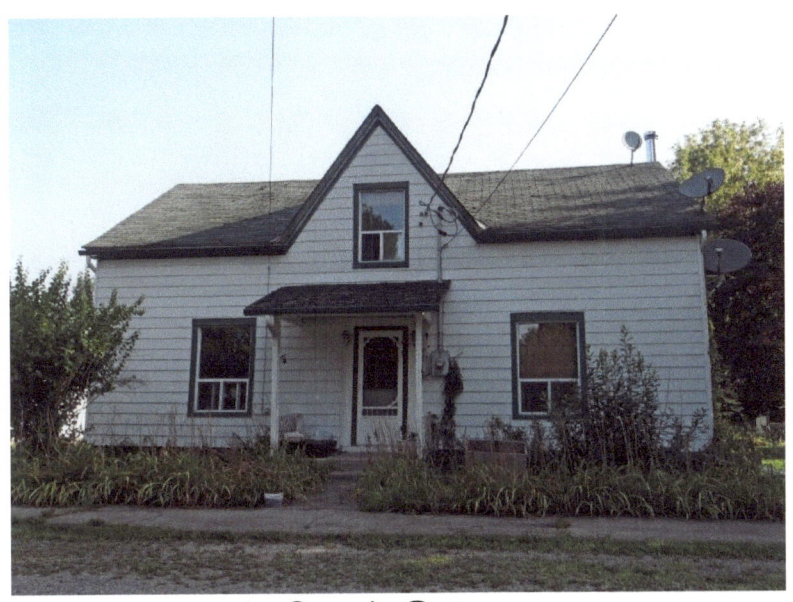

Ontario Cottage

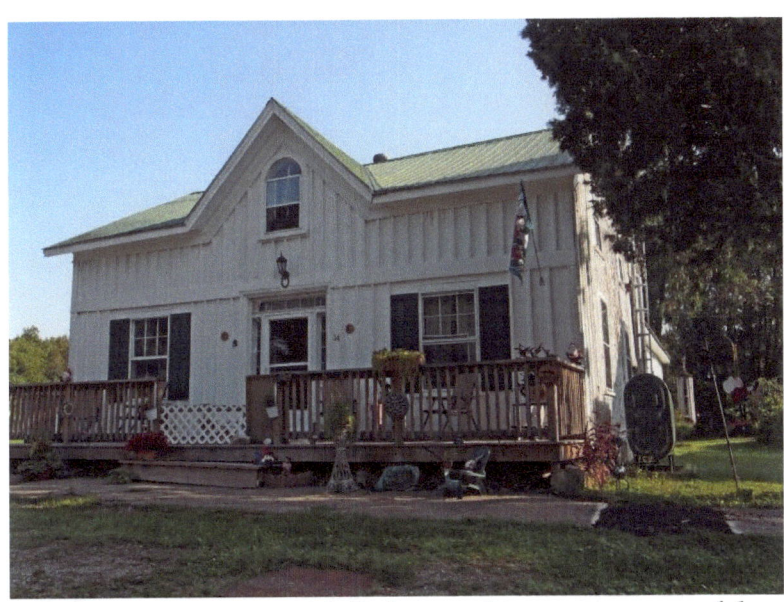

#14 - Ontario Cottage – sidelights and transom; round-headed
window in gable

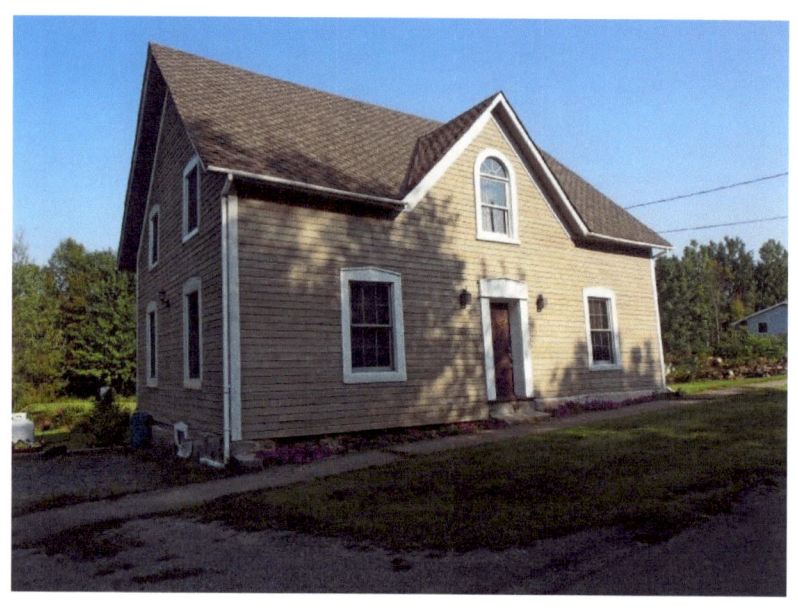

9 - Ontario Cottage – round-headed window in gable

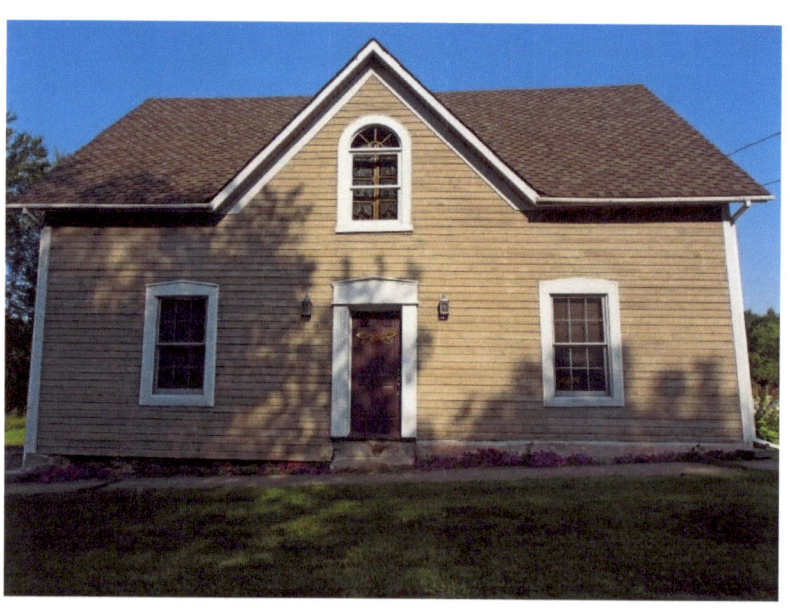

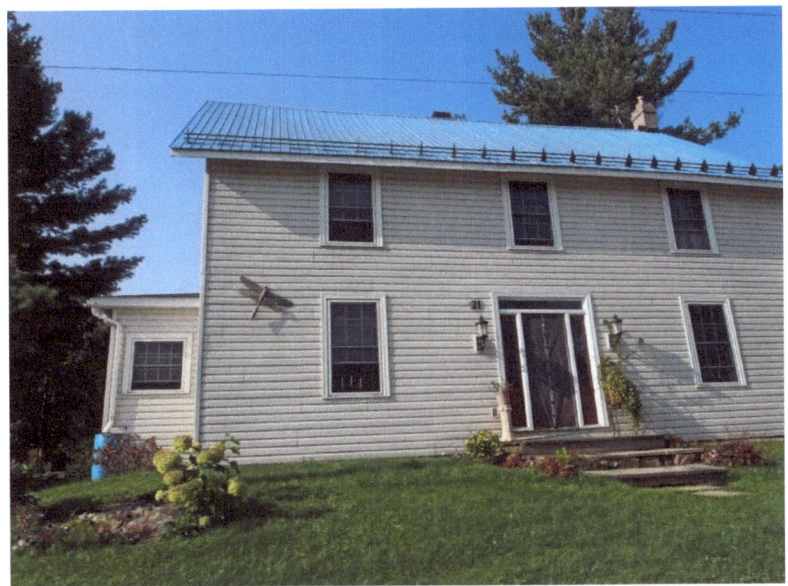

#21

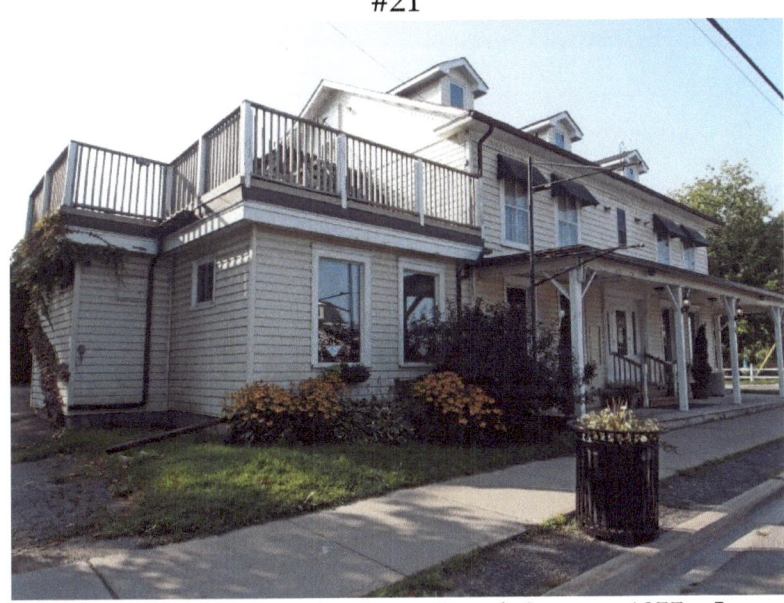

4 Drummond Street – The Stage Coach Inn – c. 1855 – James MacDonald, an early merchant in Newboro, built this home and business; in 1872 William O'Connor purchased it and converted it into "The Ontario Hotel"; later called "Landon House" (1920-1966); then the current name; Georgian style; dormers

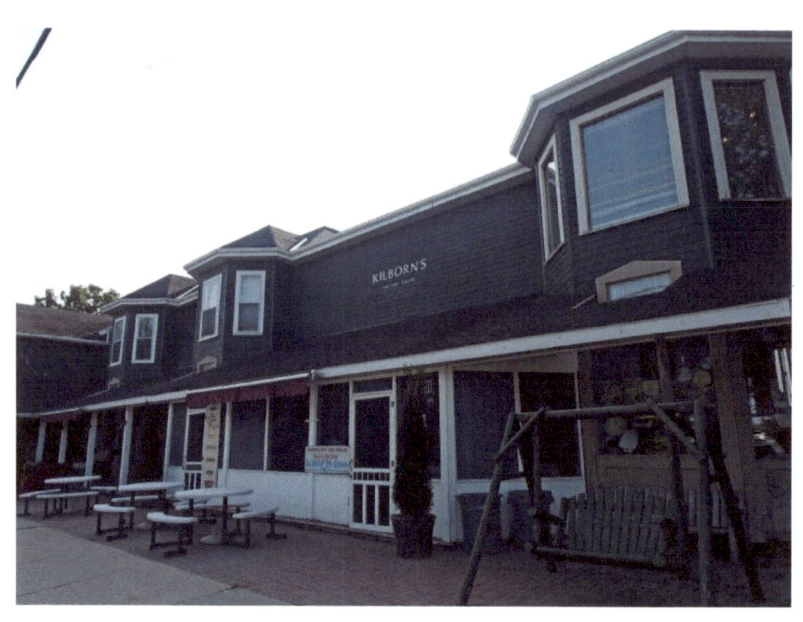

10 Drummond Street –Kilborn's on the Rideau

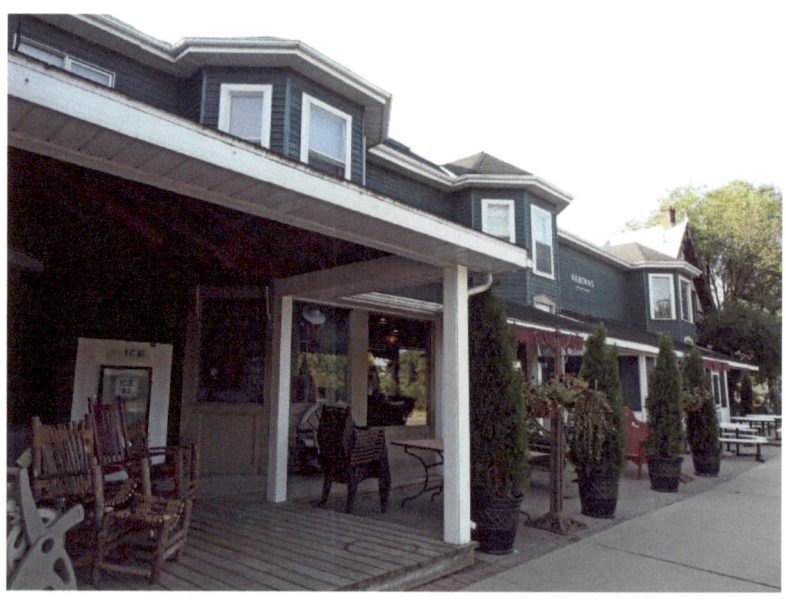

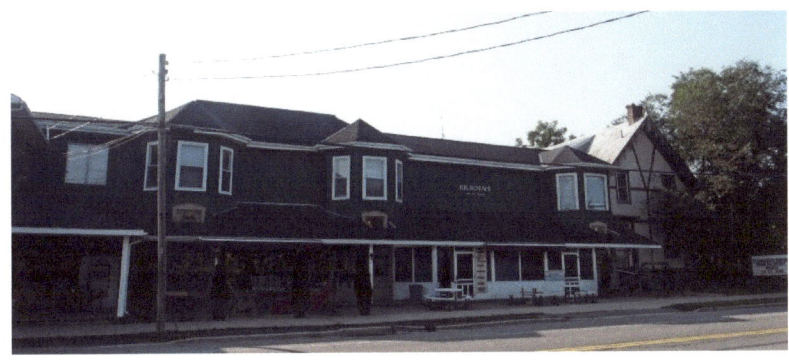

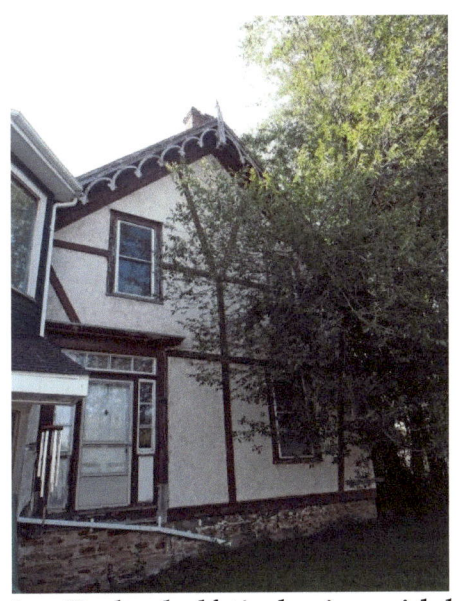

Verge board trim, Tudor half-timbering; sidelights, transom

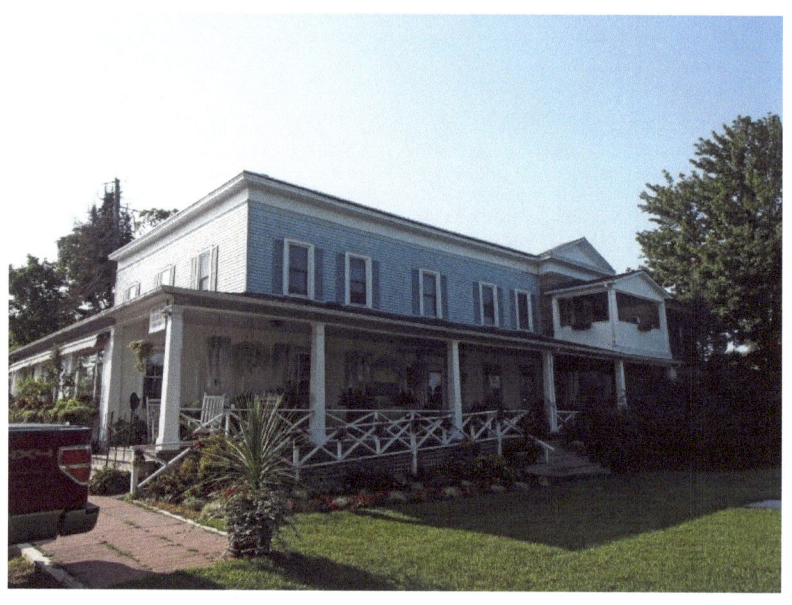

2 Drummond Street – The Colonel John Kilborn House – c. 1835 – mixed styles – far right is stone

In 1828 while living in Brockville, Colonel Kilborn was elected to Parliament; when his term expired, he declined re-election and moved to Kilmarnock. In 1852 he was postmaster in Brockville where he later successfully ran for Parliament. He retired to Newboro. He and his wife Elizabeth Sherwood had nine children – eight sons and one daughter. Colonel Kilborn died at age 93.

Architectural Terms

Banding: Different materials, colors or textures used in horizontal bands along a wall. Example: Portland United Church, Page 7	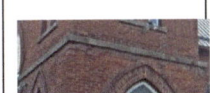
Bay Window: A window that projects out from a wall, in a semicircular, rectangular, or polygonal design. Used frequently in Gothic and Victorian designs. Example: Portland, Page 10	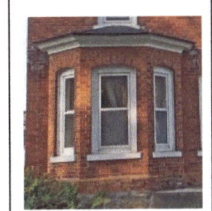
Brackets: a decorative or weight-bearing structural element which forms a right angle with one side against a wall and the other under a projecting surface such as an eave or roof. Example: 7 Drummond Street, Newboro, Pg. 34	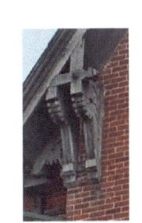
Buttress: a masonry structure built against or projecting from a wall which serves to support or reinforce the wall. In Canadian architecture, they are sometimes used for decoration. Example: Portland United Church, Page 7	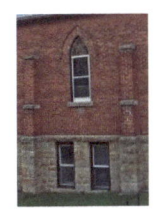
Capital: The uppermost finish or decoration on a column. A Doric column is characterized by a plain column with no base, a shaft with twenty flutings, and a simple capital with a simple entablature. Example: 5 Main Street, Newboro, Page 48	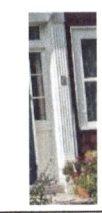

Cobblestone architecture: Refers to the use of cobblestones embedded in mortar as a method for erecting walls on houses and commercial buildings. Example: Newboro, Page 43	
Columns were initially created to support a roof and porch structure. Originally they were free standing. Over time, builders began to build the walls between the columns so that the columns were part of the wall itself. These are called engaged columns. Engaged columns can be either structural or decorative. Example: 5 Main Street, Newboro, Page 48	
Cornice Return: decorative element on the end of a gable. Example: Portland, Page 18	
Course: continuous horizontal row or layer of stone or brick. Example: 24 Drummond Street, Newboro, Page 31	
Dentil Moulding: an even series of rectangles used as ornamental decoration in cornices. Example: #18, Newboro, Page 38	
Dichromatic brickwork: the use of two colors of brick, tile or slate to decorate a façade. Polychromatic is the use of more than two colors. Example: 7 Drummond Street, Newboro, Page 33	

Dormer: (French for "sleep") a gable end window that pierces through the plane of a sloping roof surface to create usable space in the top floor or attic of a building by adding headroom. Example: 9 Drummond Street, Newboro, Page 32	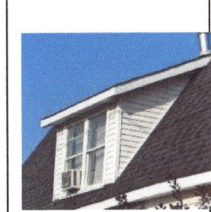
Fretwork: interlaced decorative design resembling a bracket. Example: 22 Drummond Street, Newboro, Page 32	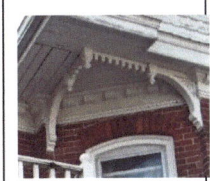
Gable: the triangular portion of a wall between the edges of a sloping roof. Example: 17 East Water Street, Portland, Page 14	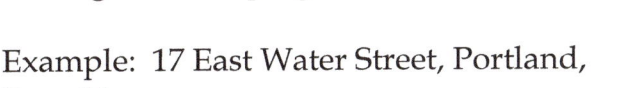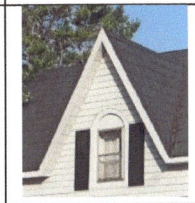
Gambrel Roof: a symmetrical two-sided roof with two slopes on each side; the upper slope is positioned at a shallow angle, while the lower slope is steep. It is similar to a mansard roof, but a gambrel has vertical gable ends instead of being hipped at the four corners of the building. Example: 9 Drummond St., Newboro, Page 32	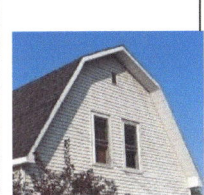
Hip Roof: a roof where all sides slope downwards to the walls with no gables. Example: Portland, Page 20	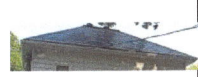

Keystones and Voussoirs: a voussoir is a wedge-shaped element used in building an arch. A keystone is the central stone that locks all the stones into position, allowing the arch to bear weight. A keystone is often enlarged and embellished. Example: Portland, Page 13	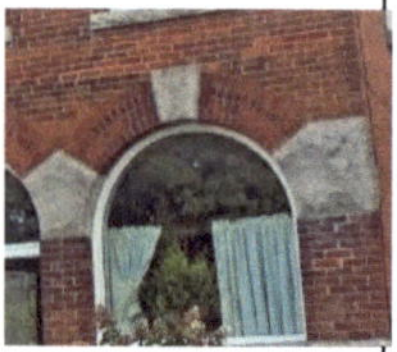
Lancet Window: a tall, narrow window with a pointed arch at its top. Example: 26 Drummond Street, Newboro, Page 30	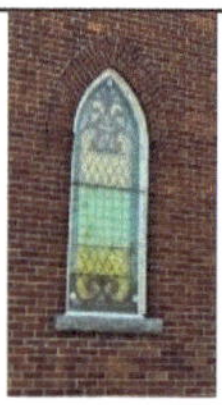
Lintel: horizontal part above a window or door that supports the structure above it. Example: 7 Drummond Street, Newboro, Page 34	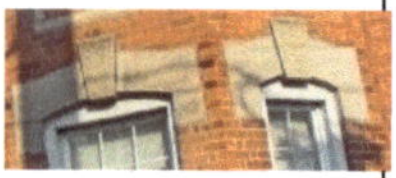
Mansard Roof: This style was popularized by Francois Mansart (1598-1666), an accomplished architect of the French Baroque period and especially fashionable during the Second French Empire (1852-1870). This roof is almost flat on the top section, with two slopes on each of its sides with the lower slope at a steeper angle than the upper and having dormer windows. Example: #31, Newboro, Page 28	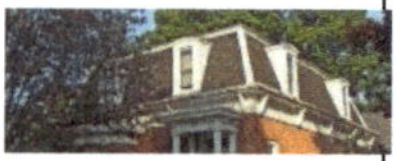
Quoin: masonry blocks at the corner of a wall, often a decorative feature, usually larger or of a different colour than the rest of the wall. Example: Portland, Page 6	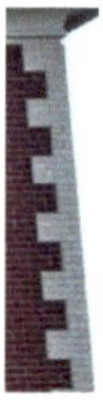

Sidelight: a vertical window that flanks a door, and is often used to emphasize the importance of a primary entrance. **Transom Window:** the light above the doorway, also called a fanlight. Example: 5 Main Street, Newboro, Page 48	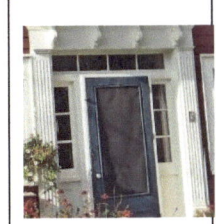
Tower: A circular, square, or octagonal vertical structure higher than the surrounding structure that is usually part of an existing building and is created either for extra defense or for a specific purpose such as a clock or a bell tower. Example: 15 Brock Street, Newboro, Page 37	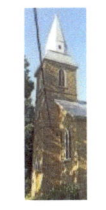
Verge board and Finial: also called bargeboards – hang from the projecting end of a roof and are often elaborately carved and ornamented. Example: Portland, Page 19	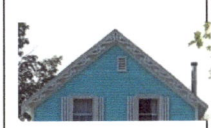

Classical Revival, 1820-1860 – This style was an analytical, scientific, and dogmatic revival based on intensive studies of Greek and Roman buildings, concerned with the application of Greek plans and proportions to civic buildings. Schools, libraries, government offices, and most other civic buildings were built in the Classical Revival style. The white columned porches of the Classical Revival domestic buildings are identified with the mansions of wealthy land owners in Canada. Example: 5 Main Street, Newboro, Page 48	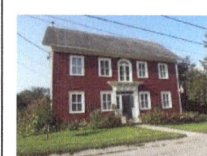
Edwardian, 1900-1930 – This style bridges the ornate and elaborate styles of the Victorian era and the simplified styles of the 20th century. Edwardian Classicism provided simple, balanced facades, simple rooflines, dormer windows, large front porches, and smooth brick surfaces. Voussoirs and keystones are used sparingly and are understated. Finials and cresting are absent. Cornice brackets and braces are block-like and openings have flat arches or plain stone lintels. Example: Portland, Page 14	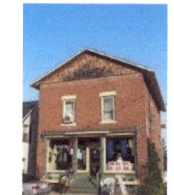
Georgian, before 1860 – This style began with the British King Georges in the 18th century. These buildings have balanced facades around a central door, medium-pitched gable roofs, and small paned windows. Example: Portland, Page 6	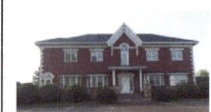

Gothic Revival, 1830-1890 – These decorative buildings have sharply-pitched gables with highly detailed verge boards, pointed-arch window openings, and dichromatic brickwork. It is a common style in Ontario. Example: 35 Colborne Street, Portland, Page 22	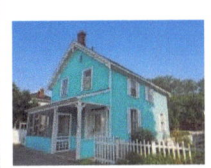
Italianate, 1850-1900 – A two story rectangular building with a mild hip roof, a projecting frontispiece, and generous eaves with ornate cornice brackets was the basis of the style; often there are large sash windows, quoins, ornate detailing on the windows, belvederes and wraparound verandahs. Italianate commercial buildings often have cast iron cresting and elegant window surrounds. Example: 24 Drummond Street, Newboro, Page 21	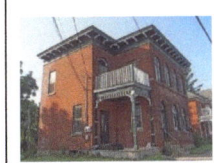
Neo-colonial (also Colonial Revival, Georgian Revival or Neo-Georgian) - Architecture from the 18th and early 19th centuries in Ontario includes a wide assortment of detailing and ornament applied to a design centered around the fireplace and the source of water. Structures are typically two storeys, have a symmetrical front facade with elaborate front doorways, often with decorative crown pediments, fanlights, and sidelights, symmetrical windows flanking the front entrance, often in pairs or threes, and columned porches. Example: 9 Drummond Street, Newboro, Page 21	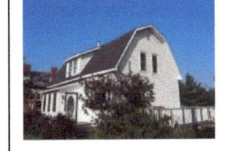

Ontario Cottage - one or one-and-a-half story buildings with a cottage or hip roof. The cottage roof is an equal hip roof where each hip extends to a point in the center of the roof. The hip roof has a long hip in the center. The Ontario Cottage is the vernacular design of the Regency Cottage which generally has a more ornate doorway and a partial or full verandah surrounding it. The roof can have a dormer, a belvedere, and generally two chimneys. Example: 14 Main Street, Newboro, Page 49	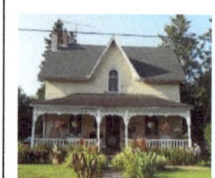
Second Empire, 1860-1880 – The mansard roof is the most noteworthy feature of this style and is evidence of the French origins. Projecting central towers and one or two-storey bays can also be present. Example: #31, Newboro, Page 27	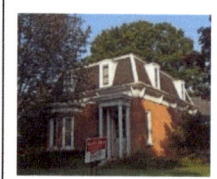
Victorian - In Ontario, a Victorian style building can be seen as any building built between 1840 and 1900 that doesn't fit into any of the other categories. It encompasses a large group of buildings constructed in brick, stone, and timber, using an eclectic mixture of Classical and Gothic motifs. Example: Newboro, Page 28	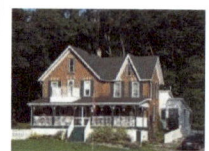

www.ingramcontent.com/pod-product-compliance
Lightning Source LLC
Chambersburg PA
CBHW040845180526
45159CB00001B/319